KNITS
from an
ENGLISH
ROSE

KNITS *from an* ENGLISH ROSE

25 *modern-vintage accessories*

L O U I S A   H A R D I N G

sixth&springbooks NEW YORK

161 Avenue of the Americas, New York, NY 10013
sixthandspringbooks.com

Editorial Director
JOY AQUILINO

Vice President
TRISHA MALCOLM

Developmental Editor
LISA SILVERMAN

Publisher
CAROLINE KILMER

Art Director
DIANE LAMPHRON

Creative Director
JOE VIOR

Editorial Assistant
JOHANNA LEVY

Production Manager
DAVID JOINNIDES

Instructions Editor
CHRISTOPHER BAHLS

President
ART JOINNIDES

Proofreader
KRISTIN M. JONES

Chairman
JAY STEIN

Photography & Design Layout
STEPHEN JESSUP

Library of Congress Cataloging-in-Publication Data
Harding, Louisa.
  Knits from an English rose : 25 modern - vintage accessories / Louisa Harding.
      pages cm
  Summary: "Timeless, accessible, and unabashedly romantic: this collection from renowned knitwear designer Louisa Harding will charm knitters of all levels. Inspired by Edwardian style, these 25 accessories all feature Louisa's signature touches: subtle shaping, masterful and delicate stitch pattern combinations (especially cables and lace), beautiful embellishments, and exciting fibers. The fashionable, feminine projects range from capelets, collars, and cowls to gloves, hats, purses, and scarves-and include notes from Louisa." — Provided by publisher.
  ISBN: 978-1-936096-65-7 (hardback)
  1. Knitting. 2. Knitting—Patterns. I. Title.
  TT820.H2663 2013
  746.43'2—dc23
                          2013022180

Manufactured in China

1 3 5 7 9 10 8 6 4 2

First Edition

Contents

INTRODUCTION

THE DICTIONARY DEFINITION OF AN 'ENGLISH ROSE' IS AN ATTRACTIVE GIRL OR WOMAN WHOSE PRETTINESS IS CONSIDERED TO BE QUINTESSENTIALLY ENGLISH.

Over the years my knitting designs, publications and imagery have often been referred to as 'quintessentially English'. As a creative person you are the product of your life experience, education and family, mine all deeply rooted in England. Growing up in the centre of London and living in a high-rise apartment, I had no green grass or rose bush garden; my playgrounds were museums and galleries. Visiting these magical places I developed a love of costume, textiles and fashion. I learnt to sew and relished the idea that you could turn a flat piece of fabric into a three-dimensional garment. I scoured London's markets buying up fabric oddments, soon realising I was strongly attracted to shiny and embellished fabrics, anything with sequins and beads.

My education path took me to college to study 'Textiles for Fashion' in Brighton, an archetypal English seaside town, with a pier, fish and chips and stony beach as well as the best vintage shops that England has to offer. The vintage stores offered me, the humble fashion student, an alternative way to dress. Scouring racks of handmade dresses I saw the skill and love that went into making these clothes, the processes used, the attention to detail and the beauty of the embroidered embellishments. At college I discovered my love of designing using the medium of hand knitting. Although I was taught to knit by my maternal grandmother at age six, college showed me how to take the knit and purl stitches, combine and experiment with them and transform yarn into beautiful knitted garments.

During college I was fortunate to spend a three-month internship in Yorkshire at Rowan Yarns. All of a sudden, I found myself with my urban background transferred to the middle of the English countryside, green fields and country lanes, dry stone walls and an expanse of sky that went on and on uninterrupted across the horizon. I fell in love with Yorkshire, the wide-open spaces, the flora and fauna, the amazingly friendly people, and I decided to move there after college, leaving behind my London city life. Yorkshire is the largest county in England, its symbol the white Tudor Rose. In our house we have a stained-glass window depicting this heraldic emblem and little wild roses grow all around our garden which is a rambling place filled with native English flowers.

Knits from an English Rose encapsulates my style, a style that has evolved over time stimulated by all my jumbled influences; the girl who grew up in urban London and found herself in the wildness of Yorkshire. My designs are inspired by my love of fashion, costume and vintage clothing; my yarns are chosen for their elegance, sparkle, beautiful construction and fabulous colour. I strongly believe that whatever age we may be we all have an inner girl, and for me she is the ever elusive ideal of the 'English Rose', feminine, individual and creative. The designs and images in this book are a visualisation of my 'English Rose' narrative, inspired by and photographed at Cannon Hall, a wonderful house steeped in heritage and set in the beautiful Yorkshire landscape.

CARRIE
ROSETTE SHAWL
PATTERN PAGE 26

Ada
Clutch Purse
pattern page 32

BETTE
BOW BERET
PATTERN PAGE 36

ASTRID
WHISPERY SCARF
PATTERN PAGE 40

LORETTA
ELEGANT COLLAR

MABEL
CHEEKY MITTENS

FLORA
WILD ROSE PURSE

PEGGY
PRETTY COLLAR

LULU
LACY CAPELET
PATTERN PAGE 60

ESTELLE
FERN BOBBLE SCARF
PATTERN PAGE 66

FAYE
RUBY BERET
PATTERN PAGE 70

MYRTLE
FUR COLLAR
PATTERN PAGE 74

LOLA
CHIC LITTLEPURSE
PATTERN PAGE 78

CONSTANCE
ROSE BUD MITTENS
PATTERN PAGE 82

AGNES
PRINCESS CAPE
PATTERN PAGE 86

MURIEL
PAISLEY CAPELET
PATTERN PAGE 90

EVELYN
GLAMOROUS BOBBLE HAT
pattern page 96

EVELYN
GLAMOROUS BOBBLE HAT
PATTERN PAGE 96

LAVERNE
BEAUTIFUL BLOOM SCARF
PATTERN PAGE 100

LAVERNE
BEAUTIFUL BLOOM SCARF
PATTERN PAGE 100

IRMA
FLIRTY HAT
PATTERN PAGE 104

WINNIE
FLIRTY BOBBLE HAT
PATTERN PAGE 108

Winnie
Flirty Bobble Hat
pattern page 108

EUNICE
CORONET CAPELET
PATTERN PAGE 112

HATTIE
ELEGANT MITTENS
PATTERN PAGE 118

HATTIE
ELEGANT MITTENS
PATTERN PAGE 118

BONNIE
BUTTERFLY VEST
PATTERN PAGE 124

VELMA
WISPY SHRUG
PATTERN PAGE 128

NORA
DAZZLE SCARF
PATTERN PAGE 132

NORA
DAZZLE SCARF
PATTERN PAGE 132

CARRIE
ROSETTE SHAWL

When I design, sometimes the idea for the project comes from knitting a swatch, other times from a sketch. 'Carrie' began life as a sketch, the difficulty with this being how to make my hand-knitted fabric resemble my drawing. As a result, I love this design: I had to push my creative and technical abilities and feel I have created a timeless, elegant shawl that embodies my idea of 'English Rose'.

ONE SIZE
Approx. 21.5 cm (8½ in) wide x 146 cm (57½ in) long

YARN
3
Knitted in Double Knitting–weight yarn
Photographed using 3 x 50g/110m (1.75oz/120yd) hanks of Louisa Harding *Orielle* in 24 Cerise

NEEDLES
Pair of 4.5 mm (US 7) knitting needles

TENSION/GAUGE
20 sts x 28 rows to 10 cm (4 in) square measured over lace patt using 4.5 mm (US 7) knitting needles.

EXTRAS
Button and brooch back for rosette

SPECIAL ABBREVIATIONS
SSK – slip 2 sts knitwise one at a time from the LH needle to the RH needle,
insert LH needle tip through both front loops and knit together. SSM – slip stitch marker.
Make scallop – using first stitch on LH needle cast on 6 sts, knit the first st,
(this stitch is not worked again until patt row 8), cast off the next 5 sts knitwise,
so last stitch cast off is the same stitch used to cast on, (2 sts on RH needle).
Join scallop – slip stitch on RH needle onto LH needle, K this together with first stitch on
LH needle, scallop made (1 st on RH needle).

Carrie Rosette Shawl

Rosette
Using 4.5 mm (US 7) circular needle cast on 222 sts.
Row 1: Knit.
Row 2: K2, (K1, slip this st back onto LH needle, lift the next 8 sts on LH needle over this st and off needle, knit the first st again, K2) 20 times. (62 sts)

Now work short row shaping as folls:
Row 3: K54, wrap next st, turn work.
Row 4: Knit.
Row 5: K46, wrap next st, turn work.
Row 6: Knit.
Row 7: K38, wrap next st, turn work.
Row 8: Knit.
Row 9: K30, wrap next st, turn work.
Row 10: Knit.
Row 11: K22, wrap next st, turn work.
Row 12: Knit.
Row 13: K14, wrap next st, turn work.
Row 14: Knit.

Making up
Cut yarn and thread through sts on needle, pull tightly to create a rosette, secure with a few stitches and add a button to the rosette centre.
Stitch brooch back to reverse of rosette.

Shawl
Using 4.5 mm (US 7) needles cast on 10 sts.
Foundation row 1 (RS): Knit.
Foundation row 2: Knit.

Work in patt with scallop edging increasing sts as folls:

Row 1 (RS)(inc): K2, (yo, K2tog) 3 times, place a stitch marker, yo, K2. (11 sts)
Row 2: Make scallop – using first stitch on LH needle cast on 6 sts, knit the first st, (this stitch is not worked again until patt row 8), cast off the next 5 sts knitwise, so last stitch cast off is the same stitch used to cast on, (2 sts on RH needle), P2, SSM - slip stitch marker, K8.
Row 3: K8, SSM, K3. (1 stitch on LH needle)
Row 4: (1 st on RH needle) K1, P2, SSM, K8.

Row 5 (inc): K2, (yo, K2tog) 3 times, SSM, K1, yo, K2.
(12 sts + 1 stitch on LH needle)
Row 6: (1 stitch on RH needle) K1, P3, SSM, K8.
Row 7: K8, SSM, K4. (1 stitch on LH needle)
Row 8: Join scallop - slip stitch on RH needle onto LH needle, K this together with first stitch on LH needle, scallop made, P3, SSM, K8. (12 sts)

Row 9 (inc): K2, (yo, K2tog) 3 times, SSM, K2, yo, K2. (13 sts)
Row 10: Make scallop - (2 sts on RH needle), P4, SSM, K8.
Row 11: K8, SSM, K5. (1 stitch on LH needle)
Row 12: (1 st on RH needle) K1, P4, SSM, K8.

Row 13 (inc): K2, (yo, K2tog) 3 times, SSM, K3, yo, K2.
(14 sts + 1 stitch on LH needle)
Row 14: (1 stitch on RH needle) K1, P5, SSM, K8.
Row 15: K8, SSM, K6. (1 stitch on LH needle)
Row 16: Join scallop, (1 st on RH needle), P5, SSM, K8.
(14 sts)

Work in patt as set introducing lace patt and working scallop edging increasing sts as folls:

Row 17 (inc): K2, (yo, K2tog) 3 times, SSM, K2, yo, SSK, yo, K2. (15 sts)
Row 18: Make scallop - (2 sts on RH needle), P6, SSM, K8.
Row 19: K8, SSM, K2tog, yo, K1, yo, SSK, K2.
(1 stitch on LH needle)
Row 20: (1 st on RH needle) K1, P6, SSM, K8.

Row 21 (inc): K2, (yo, K2tog) 3 times, SSM, K2, yo, SSK, K1, yo, K2. (16 sts + 1 stitch on LH needle)
Row 22: (1 stitch on RH needle) K1, P7, SSM, K8.
Row 23: K8, SSM, K8. (1 stitch on LH needle)
Row 24: Join scallop, (1 st on RH needle), P7, SSM, K8.
(16 sts)

Row 25 (inc): K2, (yo, K2tog) 3 times, SSM, K2, yo, SSK, K2, yo, K2. (17 sts)
Row 26: Make scallop - (2 sts on RH needle), P8, SSM, K8.
Row 27: K8, SSM, K2tog, yo, K1, yo, SSK, K4.
(1 stitch on LH needle)
Row 28: (1 st on RH needle) K1, P8, SSM, K8.

Row 29 (inc): K2, (yo, K2tog) 3 times, SSM, K2, yo, SSK, K3, yo, K2. (18 sts + 1 stitch on LH needle)
Row 30: (1 stitch on RH needle) K1, P9, SSM, K8.
Row 31: K8, SSM, K10. (1 stitch on LH needle)
Row 32: Join scallop, (1 st on RH needle), P9, SSM, K8.
(18 sts)

Row 33 (inc): K2, (yo, K2tog) 3 times, SSM, K2, yo, SSK, K4, yo, K2. (19 sts)
Row 34: Make scallop - (2 sts on RH needle), P10, SSM, K8.
Row 35: K8, SSM, K2tog, yo, K1, yo, SSK, K6.
(1 stitch on LH needle)
Row 36: (1 st on RH needle) K1, P10, SSM, K8.

Row 37 (inc): K2, (yo, K2tog) 3 times, SSM, K2, yo, SSK, K5, yo, K2. (20 sts + 1 stitch on LH needle)
Row 38: (1 stitch on RH needle) K1, P11, SSM, K8.

Row 39: K8, SSM, K12. (1 stitch on LH needle)
Row 40: Join scallop, (1 st on RH needle), P11, SSM, K8. (20 sts)

Row 41 (inc): K2, (yo, K2tog) 3 times, SSM, K2, yo, SSK, K4, yo, SSK, yo, K2. (21 sts)
Row 42: Make scallop - (2 sts on RH needle), P12, SSM, K8.
Row 43: K8, SSM, (K2tog, yo, K1, yo, SSK, K1) twice, K1. (1 stitch on LH needle)
Row 44: (1 st on RH needle) K1, P12, SSM, K8.

Row 45 (inc): K2, (yo, K2tog) 3 times, SSM, (K2, yo, SSK, K2) twice, K1, yo, K2. (22 sts + 1 stitch on LH needle)
Row 46: (1 stitch on RH needle) K1, P13, SSM, K8.
Row 47: K8, SSM, K14. (1 stitch on LH needle)
Row 48: Join scallop, (1 st on RH needle), P13, SSM, K8. (22 sts)

Row 49 (inc): K2, (yo, K2tog) 3 times, SSM, (K2, yo, SSK, K2) twice, yo, K2. (23 sts)
Row 50: Make scallop - (2 sts on RH needle), P14, SSM, K8.
Row 51: K8, SSM, (K2tog, yo, K1, yo, SSK, K1) twice, K3. (1 stitch on LH needle)
Row 52: (1 st on RH needle) K1, P14, SSM, K8.

Row 53 (inc): K2, (yo, K2tog) 3 times, SSM, (K2, yo, SSK, K2) twice, K1, yo, K2. (24 sts + 1 stitch on LH needle)
Row 54: (1 stitch on RH needle) K1, P15, SSM, K8.
Row 55: K8, SSM, K16. (1 stitch on LH needle)
Row 56: Join scallop, (1 st on RH needle), P15, SSM, K8. (24 sts)

Row 57 (inc): K2, (yo, K2tog) 3 times, SSM, (K2, yo, SSK, K2) twice, K2, yo, K2. (25 sts)
Row 58: Make scallop - (2 sts on RH needle), P16, SSM, K8.
Row 59: K8, SSM, (K2tog, yo, K1, yo, SSK, K1) twice, K5. (1 stitch on LH needle)
Row 60: (1 st on RH needle) K1, P16, SSM, K8.

Row 61 (inc): K2, (yo, K2tog) 3 times, SSM, (K2, yo, SSK, K2) twice, K3, yo, K2. (26 sts + 1 stitch on LH needle)
Row 62: (1 stitch on RH needle) K1, P17, SSM, K8.
Row 63: K8, SSM, K18. (1 stitch on LH needle)
Row 64: Join scallop, (1 st on RH needle), P17, SSM, K8. (26 sts)

Starting at row 41 the last 24 rows form the lace increase patt repeat.

Cont to work in patt as set increasing every 4 rows and introducing extra lace patt every 24 rows to 46 sts ending with patt row 144.

Row 145: K2, (yo, K2tog) 3 times, SSM, (K2, yo, SSK, K2) 5 times, K2, yo, SSK, K1 yo, K2tog, K1. (46 sts)
Row 146: Make scallop - (2 sts on RH needle), P37, SSM, K8.
Row 147: K8, SSM, (K2tog, yo, K1, yo, SSK, K1) 6 times, K2. (1 stitch on LH needle)
Row 148: (1 st on RH needle) K1, P37, SSM, K8.
Row 149: K2, (yo, K2tog) 3 times, SSM, (K2, yo, SSK, K2) 5 times, K2, yo, SSK, K1, yo, K2tog, K1. (46 sts + 1 stitch on LH needle)
Row 150: (1 stitch on RH needle) K1, P37, SSM, K8.
Row 152: K8, SSM, K38. (1 stitch on LH needle)
Row 153: Join scallop, (1 st on RH needle), P37, SSM, K8. (46 sts)

The last 8 rows form the lace and edging patt. Work these 8 rows 17 times more.

Now work shawl decreases as folls:

Dec row 1 (RS)(dec): K2, (yo, K2tog) 3 times, SSM, (K2, yo, SSK, K2) 5 times, K3, K2tog, yo, K2tog, K1. (45 sts)
Dec row 2: Make scallop - (2 sts on RH needle), P36, SSM, K8.
Dec row 3: K8, SSM, (K2tog, yo, K1, yo, SSK, K1) 5 times, K7. (1 stitch on LH needle)
Dec row 4: (1 st on RH needle) K1, P36, SSM, K8.

Dec row 5 (dec): K2, (yo, K2tog) 3 times, SSM, (K2, yo, SSK, K2) 5 times, K2, K2tog, yo, K2tog, K1. (44 sts + 1 stitch on LH needle)
Dec row 6: (1 stitch on RH needle) K1, P35, SSM, K8.
Dec row 7: K8, SSM, K36. (1 stitch on LH needle)
Dec row 8: Join scallop, (1 st on RH needle), P35, SSM, K8. (44 sts)

Dec row 9 (dec): K2, (yo, K2tog) 3 times, SSM, (K2, yo, SSK, K2) 5 times, K1, K2tog, yo, K2tog, K1. (43 sts)
Dec row 10: Make scallop - (2 sts on RH needle), P34, SSM, K8.
Dec row 11: K8, SSM, (K2tog, yo, K1, yo, SSK, K1) 5 times, K5. (1 stitch on LH needle)
Dec row 12: (1 st on RH needle) K1, P34, SSM, K8.

Dec row 13 (dec): K2, (yo, K2tog) 3 times, SSM, (K2, yo, SSK, K2) 5 times, K2tog, yo, K2tog, K1. (42 sts + 1 stitch on LH needle)
Dec row 14: (1 stitch on RH needle) K1, P33, SSM, K8.
Dec row 15: K8, SSM, K34. (1 stitch on LH needle)
Dec row 16: Join scallop, (1 st on RH needle), P33, SSM, K8. (42 sts)

Dec row 17 (dec): K2, (yo, K2tog) 3 times, SSM, (K2, yo, SSK, K2) 4 times, K2, yo, SSK, K1, K2tog, yo, K2tog, K1. (41 sts)

Dec row 18: Make scallop - (2 sts on RH needle), P32, SSM, K8.

Dec row 19: K8, SSM, (K2tog, yo, K1, yo, SSK, K1) 5 times, K3. (1 stitch on LH needle)

Dec row 20: (1 st on RH needle) K1, P32, SSM, K8.

Dec row 21 (dec): K2, (yo, K2tog) 3 times, SSM, (K2, yo, SSK, K2) 4 times, K2, yo, SSK, K2tog, yo, K2tog, K1. (40 sts + 1 stitch on LH needle)

Dec row 22: (1 stitch on RH needle) K1, P31, SSM, K8.

Dec row 23: K8, SSM, K32. (1 stitch on LH needle)

Dec row 24: Join scallop, (1 st on RH needle), P31, SSM, K8. (40 sts)

Starting at dec row 1 the last 24 rows form the lace decrease patt repeat.

Cont to work in patt as set decreasing every 4 rows until 11 sts remain ending with RS facing for next row.
Work 2 rows in garter st.
Cast off.

MAKING UP
Sew in all ends.
Press/block shawl as described on page 138.

ADA
Clutch Purse

Designed to add glamour, this clutch purse has an aura of a bygone age. A beautiful object can turn heads when worked in a combination of two yarns, one of which is twinkling and self-beaded. This project knits quickly; both strands held together produce a chunky-weight yarn and the lace stitch pattern is engineered to create interest at the purse opening. To be truly glamorous takes little effort, and this purse, knit with interestingly beautiful yarns, echoes that simple, elegant ethos.

ONE SIZE
Approx. 30.5 cm (12 in) wide x 16.5 cm (6½ in) long

YARN
3
Knitted using two Double Knitting–weight yarns held together
Photographed using Louisa Harding *Grace Silk & Wool* and *Grace Hand Beaded*
A. 2 x 50g/100m (1.75oz/109yd) balls of *Grace Silk & Wool* in 41 India
B. 3 x 50g/68m (1.75oz/74yd) hanks of *Grace Hand Beaded* in 18 India

NEEDLES
Pair of 6 mm (US 10) knitting needles

TENSION/GAUGE
14 sts x 21 rows to 10 cm (4 in) square measured over st st
using 6 mm (US 8) knitting needles and both yarns held together.

SPECIAL ABBREVIATIONS
S2K1P – slip 2 sts together from LH needle to RH needle (as if knitting them together),
K1, pass the 2 slipped stitches over the stitch knitted.
SSK – slip 2 sts knitwise one at a time from the LH needle to the RH needle,
insert LH needle tip through both front loops and knit together.

Ada Clutch Purse

Using 6 mm (US 10) needles and both yarns held together cast on 49 sts.

Work 2 rows in garter st.

Now work 24 rows in patt setting sts as folls:

Patt row 1 (RS): K9, yo, K2tog, yo, K1, yo, K4, S2K1P, K4, yo, S2K1P, yo, K4, S2K1P, K4, yo, K1, yo, SSK, yo, K9.

Patt rows 2, 4, 6, 8, 10, 12, 14, 16 & 18: K5, P39, K5.

Patt row 3: K9, yo, K2tog, (yo, K3) twice, S2K1P, K3, yo, S2K1P, yo, K3, S2K1P, (K3, yo) twice, SSK, yo, K9.

Patt row 5: K9, yo, K2tog, yo, K5, yo, K2, S2K1P, K2, yo, S2K1P, yo, K2, S2K1P, K2, yo, K5, yo, SSK, yo, K9.

Patt row 7: K9, yo, K2tog, yo, K7, yo, K1, S2K1P, K1, yo, S2K1P, yo, K1, S2K1P, K1, yo, K7, yo, SSK, yo, K9.

Patt row 9: K9, yo, K2tog, yo, K9, (yo, S2K1P) 3 times, yo, K9, yo, SSK, yo, K9.

Patt row 11: K9, yo, K2tog, yo, K10, K2tog, yo, S2K1P, yo, SSK, K10, yo, SSK, yo, K9.

Patt row 13: K9, yo, K2tog, yo, K1, yo, K4, S2K1P, K4, yo, S2K1P, yo, K4, S2K1P, K4, yo, K1, yo, SSK, yo, K9.

Patt row 15: K9, yo, K2tog, (yo, K3) twice, S2K1P, K3, yo, S2K1P, yo, K3, S2K1P, (K3, yo) twice, SSK, yo, K9.

Patt row 17: K9, yo, K2tog, yo, K5, yo, K2, S2K1P, K2, yo, S2K1P, yo, K2, S2K1P, K2, yo, K5, yo, SSK, yo, K9.

Patt row 19 (dec): K9, yo, K2tog, yo, SSK, K5, yo, K1, S2K1P, K1, yo, S2K1P, yo, K1, S2K1P, K1, yo, K5, K2tog, yo, SSK, yo, K9. (47 sts)

Patt row 20: K5, P37, K5.

Patt row 21 (dec): K9, yo, K2tog, yo, SSK, K6, (yo, S2K1P) 3 times, yo, K6, K2tog, yo, SSK, yo, K9. (45 sts)

Patt row 22: K5, P35, K5.

Patt row 23 (dec): K9, yo, K2tog, yo, SSK, K6, K2tog, yo, S2K1P, yo, SSK, K6, K2tog, yo, SSK, yo, K9. (43 sts)

Patt row 24: K5, P33, K5.

Next row (RS): Purl to form fold line.

Next row: Purl.

Beg with a K row work 34 rows in st st, ending with RS facing for next row.

Next row (RS): Purl to form fold line.
Next row: Purl.

Beg with a K row work 29 rows in st st, ending with WS facing for next row.

Next row (WS): Knit.
Next row: Knit.
Cast off knitwise on WS.

MAKING UP
Sew in ends.
Press/block piece as described on page 138.

Using the photograph as a guide, fold over front flap at fold line, mark the position at side edge 2 rows down from fold line. Fold the cast off edge to meet the markers at side edges. With RS facing and row ends held together, sew the sides together using mattress stitch. 🌹

BETTE
Bow Beret

The subtly changing hues of the variegated yarn used for this bow-fronted beret ensure that it looks far more complex to knit than it actually is. A simple moss stitch band evolves into eyelet bands which decrease to the crown, the colours fading in and out with the pattern. A knitted bow jauntily sewn to one side makes this simple hat look all at once vintage and modern.

ONE SIZE
Approx. 56 cm (22 in) when stretched to fit

YARN
(3)
Knitted in Double Knitting–weight yarn
Photographed using 1 x 50g/250m (1.75oz/273yd) ball of Louisa Harding *Amitola* in 111 Dark Rose

NEEDLES
3.5 mm (US 4) and 4.5 mm (US 7) 60cm (24 in) circular knitting needles, (4.5 mm dpns)
Stitch marker

TENSION/GAUGE
18 sts x 32 rows to 10 cm (4 in) square measured over st st and eyelet pattern
using 4.5 mm (US 7) 60 cm (24 in) circular knitting needle.

SPECIAL ABBREVIATION
SSM – slip stitch marker.

NOTE
I find that using a stitch marker placed at the end of each round helps to identify which round is next and where the cable pattern begins and ends. I use the magic loop technique when knitting hats in the round to work the crown shaping decreases, you may find it easier to convert to double-pointed needles.

Bette Bow Beret

Using 3.5 mm (US 4) circular needle cast on 100 sts.
Foundation round 1: Knit, place stich marker.
Foundation round 2: Purl to marker, slip stitch marker - SSM.

Work 22 rounds in moss st setting sts as folls:
Round 1: (K1, P1) to end, SSM.
Round 2: (P1, K1) to end, SSM.
These 2 rounds form the moss st patt.
Rep these 2 rounds 10 times more.

Round 23: Knit to end, SSM.
Round 24: Purl to end, SSM.
Round 25 (eyelets): (yo, K2tog) 50 times, SSM.
Round 26: Purl to end, SSM.

Round 27 (inc): (K2, yo) 50 times, SSM. (150 sts)
Round 28: (P2, purl into the back of yo on previous row) 50 times, SSM.

Change to 4.5 mm (US 7) circular needle, work in st st and eyelet patt setting rounds as folls:

Patt round 1, 2, 3, 4 & 5: Knit to end, SSM.
Patt round 6: Purl to end, SSM.
Patt round 7 (eyelets): (yo, K2tog) 75 times, SSM.
Patt round 8: Purl to end, SSM.
Work the last 8 rounds three times more.

Work crown decreases as folls:
Crown round 1 (dec): (K8, K2tog) 15 times, SSM. (135 sts)
Crown round 2, 3 & 4: Knit to end, SSM.

Crown round 5 (dec): (K7, K2tog) 15 times, SSM. (120 sts)
Crown round 6: Purl to end, SSM.
Crown round 7 (eyelets): (yo, K2tog) 60 times, SSM.
Crown round 8: Purl to end, SSM.

Crown round 9 (dec): (K6, K2tog) 15 times, SSM. (105 sts)
Crown round 10, 11 & 12: Knit to end, SSM.

Crown round 13 (dec): (K5, K2tog) 15 times, SSM. (90 sts)
Crown round 14: Purl to end, SSM.
Crown round 15 (eyelets): (yo, K2tog) 45 times, SSM.
Crown round 16: Purl to end, SSM.

Crown round 17 (dec): (K4, K2tog) 15 times, SSM. (75 sts)
Crown round 18, 19, & 20: Knit to end, SSM.

Crown round 21 (dec): (K3, K2tog) 15 times, SSM. (60 sts)
Crown round 22: Purl to end, SSM.
Crown round 23 (eyelets): (yo, K2tog) 30 times, SSM.
Crown round 24: Purl to end, SSM.

Crown round 25 (dec): (K2, K2tog) 15 times, SSM. (45 sts)
Crown round 26: Knit to end, SSM.

Crown round 27 (dec): (K1, K2tog) 15 times, SSM. (30 sts)
Crown round 28: Knit to end, SSM.

Crown round 29 (dec): (K2tog) 15 times, SSM. (15 sts)
Crown round 30: Purl to end, SSM.

Crown round 31 (dec): (K2tog) 7 times, K1, SSM. (8 sts)
Break yarn, thread through rem sts, draw up and fasten off.

Bow
Using 3.5 mm (US 4) circular needle cast on 29 sts.
Foundation round 1: Knit.
Foundation round 2: (K1, P1) 6 times, (slip 1 purlwise, P1) 3 times, (K1, P1) 5 times, K1.

Work 26 rows in moss st and slip st patt setting sts as folls:
Row 1: (K1, P1) 5 times, K2, (slip 1 purlwise, K1) 3 times, (K1, P1) 6 times, K1.
Row 2: (K1, P1) 6 times, (slip 1 purlwise, P1) 3 times, (K1, P1) 5 times, K1.
These 2 rows form the patt.
Work these 2 rows 12 times more, ending with RS facing for next row.
Next row (RS): Knit.
Cast off Knit knitwise on WS.

Using the photograph as a guide sew the bow to the moss stitch band of the beret gathering the central slip stitch panel to make the centre of the bow.

Making up
Sew in ends.
Press/block beret as described on page 138. ❀

ASTRID
WHISPERY SCARF

This versatile scarf is whispery light. A simple chevron lace pattern dictates the undulating cast-on edge and the vertical striped eyelet pattern is achieved by knitting a variegated yarn sideways. This does involve casting on many, many stitches, however, as a consolation, there are only a few pattern row repeats concluding with a pretty picot cast-off. Whether this scarf is worn coiled cosily around the neck or the shoulders, its softness and loft will keep the chills at bay.

ONE SIZE
Approx. 20.5 cm (8 in) wide x 191.5 cm (75 in) long

YARN
(3)
Knitted in Double Knitting–weight yarn
Photographed using 2 x 50g/250m (1.75oz/273yd) balls of Louisa Harding *Amitola* in 103 Berries

NEEDLES
Pair of 4.5 mm (US 7) knitting needles
35 stitch markers

TENSION/GAUGE
18 sts x 32 rows to 10 cm (4 in) square measured over eyelet and stocking stitch patt
using 4.5 mm (US 7) knitting needles.

SPECIAL ABBREVIATIONS
S2KP – slip 2 sts onto RH needle as if going to knit them together, K1,
pass the 2 slipped stitches over the knitted stitch.
SSM – slip stitch marker.

NOTE
When casting on a large number of stitches I find that it helps to put in a stitch marker after every
20 sts cast on which helps with keeping the stitch count.

KNITTING WITH AMITOLA
To avoid any strong colour striping, once you have completed your first ball of yarn,
ensure the next ball you use starts with a similar colour to the one just finished.

ASTRID WHISPERY SCARF

Using 4.5 mm (US 7) needles cast on 345 sts.

Foundation row 1 (RS): Knit.

Foundation row 2 (WS)(place stitch markers): K3, place stitch marker, (K10, place stitch marker) 34 times, K2. Work 10 rows in lace and eyelet edging as folls:

Edging row 1 (RS): K2, slip stitch marker - SSM (K1, yo, K3, S2KP, K3, yo, slip stitch marker - SSM) 34 times, K3.
Edging row 2: K2, P1, SSM, (K9, P1, SSM) 34 times, K2.
Edging row 3: K2, SSM, (K2, yo, K2, S2KP, K2, yo, K1, SSM) 34 times, K3.
Edging row 4: K2, P1, SSM, (P1, K7, P2, SSM) 34 times, K2.
Edging row 5: K2, SSM, (K3, yo, K1, S2KP, K1, yo, K2, SSM) 34 times, K3.
Edging row 6: K2, P1, SSM, (P2, K5, P3, SSM) 34 times, K2.
Edging row 7: K2, SSM, (K4, yo, S2KP, yo, K3, SSM) 34 times, K3.
Edging row 8: K3, SSM, (K10, SSM) 34 times, K2.
Edging row 9: K2, SSM, ([yo, K2tog] 5 times, SSM) 34 times, yo, K2tog, K1.
Edging row 10: K3, SSM, (K10, SSM) 34 times, K2.

Now work 10 rows in lace and eyelet patt setting sts as folls:

Lace row 1 (RS): K2, SSM (K1, yo, K3, S2KP, K3, yo, SSM) 34 times, K3.
Lace row 2: K2, P1, SSM, (P10, SSM) 34 times, K2.
Lace row 3: K2, SSM, (K2, yo, K2, S2KP, K2, yo, K1, SSM) 34 times, K3.
Lace row 4: K2, P1, SSM, (P10, SSM) 34 times, K2.
Lace row 5: K2, SSM, (K3, yo, K1, S2KP, K1, yo, K2, SSM) 34 times, K3.
Lace row 6: K2, P1, SSM, (P10, SSM) 34 times, K2.
Lace row 7: K2, SSM, (K4, yo, S2KP, yo, K3, SSM) 34 times, K3.
Lace row 8: K3, SSM, (K10, SSM) 34 times, K2.
Lace row 9: K2, SSM, ([yo, K2tog] 5 times, SSM) 34 times, yo, K2tog, K1.
Lace row 10: K3, SSM, (K10, SSM) 34 times, K2.

Discarding stitch markers work in decreasing stocking stitch and eyelet stripes as folls:

Row 1 (RS): Knit.
Row 2: K2, P to last 2 sts, K2.
Work these 2 rows twice more.
Row 7: Knit.
Row 8: Knit.
Row 9 (eyelets): K2, (yo, K2tog) to last st, K1.
Row 10 (WS): Knit.

Row 11: Knit.
Row 12: K2, P to last 2 sts, K2.
Work these 2 rows once more.
Row 15: Knit.
Row 16: Knit.
Row 17 (eyelets): K2, (yo, K2tog) to last st, K1.
Row 18: Knit.
Work the last 8 rows twice more.

Row 35: Knit.
Row 36: K2, P to last 2 sts, K2.
Row 37: Knit.
Row 38: Knit.
Row 39 (eyelets): K2, (yo, K2tog) to last st, K1.
Row 40: Knit.
Work the last 6 rows once more.

Work 2 rows in garter stitch, ending with RS facing for next row.

Cast off using the picot cast off method as folls:
Cast off 5 sts, *slip st on RH needle back onto LH needle, cast on 2 sts, then cast off 7 sts, rep from * until entire shawl has been cast off.

MAKING UP
Sew in ends.
Press/block scarf as described on page 138. ◉

LORETTA
Elegant Collar

In Europe in the 1940s knitted collars became fashionable as a way of renovating or altering an existing garment while wartime rationing on fabrics, yarn and clothes was in place. I love the idea of transforming a simple cardigan, pullover or blouse with the addition of a knitted collar. It is the perfect way to practice a new knitting technique or work with an expensive yarn, such as the beaded one I have used here.

ONE SIZE
Approx. 39.5 cm (15½ in)
(neck measurement at cast off)

YARN
(4)
Knitted in Worsted-weight yarn
Photographed using Louisa Harding *Grace Hand Beaded*
1 x 50g/67.5m (1.75oz/74yd) hank of *Grace Hand Beaded* in 19 Russet

NEEDLES
Pair of 4.5 mm (US 7) knitting needles

TENSION/GAUGE
20 sts x 28 rows to 10 cm (4in) square measured over st st using 4.5 mm (US 7) knitting needles.

EXTRAS
1 small mother-of-pearl button

SPECIAL ABBREVIATIONS
SSK – slip 2 sts knitwise one at a time from the LH needle to the RH needle,
insert LH needle tip through both front loops and knit together.
SK2togP – slip 1 st, K2 stitches together, pass the slip stitch over the stitches knitted together.

Loretta Elegant Collar

Using 4.5 mm (US 7) needles and using the cable cast on method, work picot cast on as folls:

*Cast on 5 sts using the cable cast on method, cast off 2 sts, slip st on RH needle back onto LH needle (3 sts now on LH needle), rep from * 37 times more, cast on 3 sts. (117 sts)

Work 2 rows in garter st.

Now work 18 rows in patt as folls:
Patt row 1: K2, (yo, SSK, K2, yo, SSK, K3, K2tog, yo, K3) 8 times, yo, SSK, K1.

Patt row 2: K2, P113, K2.

Patt row 3: K2, (K1, yo, SSK, K2, yo, SSK, K1, K2tog, yo, K2, K2tog, yo) 8 times, K3.

Patt row 4: K2, P113, K2.

Patt row 5: K2, (K2, yo, SSK, K2, yo, S2K1P, yo, K2, K2tog, yo, K1) 8 times, K3.

Patt row 6: K2, P113, K2.

Patt row 7 (dec): K2, (K1, SSK, yo, SSK, K5, K2tog, yo, K2tog) 8 times, K3. (101 sts)

Patt row 8: K2, P97, K2.

Patt row 9: K2, (K3, yo, SSK, K3, K2tog, yo, K2) 8 times, K3.

Patt row 10: K2, P97, K2.

Patt row 11 (dec): K2, (K2, SSK, yo, SSK, K1, K2tog, yo, K2tog, K1) 8 times, K3. (85 sts)

Patt row 12: K2, P81, K2.

Patt row 13: K2, (K4, yo, S2K1P, yo, K3) 8 times, K3. (85 sts)

Patt row 14: K2, P81, K2.

Patt row 15 (dec): K2, (K5, SSK, K3) 8 times, K3. (77 sts)

Patt row 16: Knit.

Patt row 17 (buttonhole): K1, SSK, yo, knit to end.

Patt row 18: Knit.
Cast off taking care not to pull stitches too tightly.

Making up
Sew in all ends.
Press/block collar as described on page 138.
Sew a button to the left front edge opposite buttonhole on opposite side of collar. ❀

MABEL
CHEEKY MITTENS

Trimmed with fur yarn, these cheeky little mittens are reminiscent of the age when a lady was not properly dressed unless she was wearing gloves. Gloves have always had a practical nature but have also developed symbolic meanings: not only would you have clean hands, but you were also thought to have a pure heart, and a lady could show her affection or favouritism to a man by taking off her glove and offering her hand to him!

ONE SIZE
Width approx. 20 cm (8 in)
(measurement taken before thumb shaping)

YARN
Knitted in Double Knitting–weight yarn
Photographed using Louisa Harding *Grace Harmonies* and *Luzia*
A. 2 x 50g/100m (1.75oz/110yd) hanks of *Grace Harmonies* in 08 Rhythm
B. 1 x 50g/40m (1.75oz/43yd) ball of *Luzia* in 006 Mink

NEEDLES
Pair of 3.25 mm (US 3) knitting needles
Pair of 4 mm (US 6) knitting needles
Pair of 6 mm (US 10) knitting needles

TENSION/GAUGE
22 sts x 30 rows to 10 cm (4 in) square measured over st st using 4 mm (US 6) knitting needles and yarn A.

SPECIAL ABBREVIATIONS
RC – right cross – Knit next 2 stitches on LH needle together, without removing the stitches from the needle, knit the first st again, slip both stitches from needle.
SSM – slip stitch marker

NOTE
I have designed these mittens to be knitted flat then seamed.
The experienced knitter can easily convert the mittens to being knitted in the round by decreasing the stitch count by two and not including the selvedge edge stitches.

MABEL CHEEKY MITTENS

RIGHT HAND
Using 6 mm (US 10) needles and yarn B cast on 38 sts.
Edging row 1: Knit.
Edging row 2: Knit.
Edging row 3: Knit.
Edging row 4: Purl.

Change to 4 mm (US 6) needles and yarn A.
Edging row 5: Knit.
Edging row 6: Purl.
Edging row 7: Knit.
Edging row 8: Purl.

Change to 3.25 mm (US 3) needles and work 4 rows in mock cable rib as folls:
Rib row 1 (RS): K1, P1, (K2, P2) 8 times, K2, P1, K1.
Rib row 2: K2, (P2, K2) 9 times.
Rib row 3: K1, P1, (RC, P2, K2, P2) 4 times, RC, P1, K1.
Rib row 4: K2, (P2, K2) 9 times.
Rep these 4 rows 5 times more.

Change to 4mm (US 6) needles and work 4 rows in st st and mock cable rib patt setting sts as folls:
Patt row 1 (RS): K4, P2, RC, P2, K2, P2, RC, P2, K20.
Patt row 2: K1, P19, (K2, P2) 3 times, K2, P3, K1.
Patt row 3: K4, P2, K2, P2, RC, P2, K2, P2, K20.
Patt row 4: K1, P19, (K2, P2) 3 times, K2, P3, K1.
Work these 4 rows once more.*

SHAPE THUMB
Patt row 9 (RS)(inc): K4, P2, RC, P2, K2, P2, RC, P2, K2, M1, K3, M1, K15. (40 sts)
Patt row 10: K1, P21, (K2, P2) 3 times, K2, P3, K1.
Patt row 11: K4, P2, K2, P2, RC, P2, K2, P2, K22.
Patt row 12: K1, P21, (K2, P2) 3 times, K2, P3, K1.

Patt row 13 (inc): K4, P2, RC, P2, K2, P2, RC, P2, K2, M1, K5, M1, K15. (42 sts)
Patt row 14: K1, P23, (K2, P2) 3 times, K2, P3, K1.
Patt row 15: K4, P2, K2, P2, RC, P2, K2, P2, K24.
Patt row 16: K1, P23, (K2, P2) 3 times, K2, P3, K1.

Patt row 17 (inc): K4, P2, RC, P2, K2, P2, RC, P2, K2, M1, K7, M1, K15. (44 sts)
Patt row 18: K1, P25, (K2, P2) 3 times, K2, P3, K1.
Patt row 19: K4, P2, K2, P2, RC, P2, K2, P2, K26.
Patt row 20: K1, P25, (K2, P2) 3 times, K2, P3, K1.

Patt row 21 (inc): K4, P2, RC, P2, K2, P2, RC, P2, K2, M1, K9, M1, K15. (46 sts)
Patt row 22: K1, P27, (K2, P2) 3 times, K2, P3, K1.
Patt row 23: K4, P2, K2, P2, RC, P2, K2, P2, K28.
Patt row 24: K1, P27, (K2, P2) 3 times, K2, P3, K1.

Patt row 25 (inc): K4, P2, RC, P2, K2, P2, RC, P2, K2, M1, K11, M1, K15. (48 sts)
Patt row 26: K1, P29, (K2, P2) 3 times, K2, P3, K1.

DIVIDE FOR THUMB
Patt row 27: K4, P2, K2, P2, RC, P2, K2, P2, K3, slip next 11 sts onto a holder for thumb, K16. (37 sts)
Patt row 28: K1, P18, (K2, P2) 3 times, K2, P3, K1.
Patt row 29: K4, P2, RC, P2, K2, P2, RC, P2, K19.
Patt row 30: K1, P18, (K2, P2) 3 times, K2, P3, K1.
Work a further 12 rows in 4 row st st and mock cable rib patt as sts set.

Next row (dec): K4, P2, K2tog, P2, K2, P2, K2tog, P2, K19. (35 sts)
Change to 3.25 mm (US 3) needles and work 2 rows in garter st.
Cast off knitwise on WS.

THUMB
With RS facing, using 4 mm (US 6) needles and yarn A rejoin yarn to 11 sts left on holder for thumb.
Next row (RS)(inc): K into front and back of first st, K9, K into front and back of last st. (13 sts)
Beg with a P row work 6 rows in st st, ending with WS facing for next row,
Change to 3.25 mm (US 3) needles.
Work 2 rows in garter st.
Cast off knitwise on WS.

LEFT HAND
Work as for right hand mitten to *.

SHAPE THUMB
Patt row 9 (RS)(inc): K15, M1, K3, M1, K2, P2, RC, P2, K2, P2, RC, P2, K4. (40 sts)
Patt row 10: K1, P3, (K2, P2) 3 times, K2, P21, K1.
Patt row 11: K22, P2, K2, P2, RC, P2, K2, P2, K4.
Patt row 12: K1, P3, (K2, P2) 3 times, K2, P21, K1.

Patt row 13 (inc): K15, M1, K5, M1, K2, P2, RC, P2, K2, P2, RC, P2, K4. (42 sts)
Patt row 14: K1, P3, (K2, P2) 3 times, K2, P23, K1.
Patt row 15: K24, P2, K2, P2, RC, P2, K2, P2, K4.
Patt row 16: K1, P3, (K2, P2) 3 times, K2, P23, K1.

Patt row 17 (inc): K15, M1, K7, M1, K2, P2, RC, P2, K2, P2, RC, P2, K4. (44 sts)
Patt row 18: K1, P3, (K2, P2) 3 times, K2, P25, K1.
Patt row 19: K26 P2, K2, P2, RC, P2, K2, P2, K4.
Patt row 20: K1, P3, (K2, P2) 3 times, K2, P25, K1.

Patt row 21 (inc): K15, M1, K9, M1, K2, P2, RC, P2, K2, P2, RC, P2, K4. (46 sts)
Patt row 22: K1, P3, (K2, P2) 3 times, K2, P27, K1.
Patt row 23: K28, P2, K2, P2, RC, P2, K2, P2, K4.
Patt row 24: K1, P3, (K2, P2) 3 times, K2, P27, K1.

Patt row 25 (inc): K15, M1, K11, M1, K2, P2, RC, P2, K2, P2, RC, P2, K4. (48 sts)
Patt row 26: K1, P3, (K2, P2) 3 times, K2, P29, K1.

DIVIDE FOR THUMB
Patt row 27: K16, slip next 11 sts onto a holder for thumb, K3, P2, K2, P2, RC, P2, K2, P2, K4. (37 sts)
Patt row 28: K1, P3, (K2, P2) 3 times, K2, P18, K1.
Patt row 29: K19, P2, RC, P2, K2, P2, RC, P2, K4.
Patt row 30: K1, P3, (K2, P2) 3 times, K2, P18, K1.
Work a further 12 rows in 4 row st st and mock cable rib patt as sts set.

Next row (dec): K19, P2, K2tog, P2, K2, P2, K2tog, P2, K4. (35 sts)
Change to 3.25 mm (US 3) needles and work 2 rows in garter st.
Cast off knitwise on WS.

THUMB
With RS facing, using 4 mm (US 6) needles and yarn A rejoin yarn to 11 sts left on holder for thumb.
Next row (RS)(inc): K into front and back of first st, K9, K into front and back of last st. (13 sts)
Beg with a P row work 6 rows in st st, ending with WS facing for next row,
Change to 3.25 mm (US 3) needles.
Work 2 rows in garter st.
Cast off knitwise on WS.

MAKING UP
Sew in all ends.
Sew side seams together using mattress stitch or back stitch if preferred, taking knit stitch selvedge into seam. Join thumb seam ensuring that the base of thumb is joined to main mitten. ◉

FLORA
WILD ROSE PURSE

Taking my inspiration from vintage handbags and purses, I designed this project to reflect the ethos of making things unique to you. The basis of this purse is very straightforward: a herringbone border provides strength for the handles; a striped moss stitch fabric gives stability for adding embellishment. Look to vintage finds to fuel your imagination and make this purse uniquely your own.

ONE SIZE
Width at opening approx. 56 cm (22 in) Length approx. 33 cm (13 in)

YARN
(4)
Knitted in Aran-weight yarn Photographed using Louisa Harding *Akiko*
2 x 50g/90m (1.75 oz/98 yd) balls each of *Akiko* in **A.** 13 Currant **B.** 16 Lavender **C.** 10 Girly
Use all yarn held double

NEEDLES
7 mm (US 10½) 80 cm (32 in) circular knitting needle
Pair of 4.5 mm (US 7) knitting needles   Stitch marker

TENSION/GAUGE
13 sts x 20 rows to 10 cm (4 in) square measured over moss st using 7 mm (US 10½)
circular knitting needle and yarn held double.

EXTRAS
Pair of leather 45.5 cm (18 in) bag handles

SPECIAL ABBREVIATIONS
SSK – slip 2 sts knitwise one at a time from the LH needle to the RH needle,
insert LH needle tip through both front loops and knit together.
S2K1P – slip 2 sts together from LH needle to RH needle (as if knitting them together),
K1, pass the 2 slipped stitches over the stitch knitted.   SSM – Slip stitch marker.

NOTE
I find that using a stitch marker placed at the end of each round helps to identify
which round is next and where the lace pattern begins and ends.

FLORA WILD ROSE PURSE

Using 7 mm (US 10½) circular needle and yarn A (held double) cast on 70 sts.
Foundation round 1: Knit, place stitch marker.
Foundation round 2: Purl, SSM – slip stitch marker.
Foundation round 3 (inc): (K4, M1, K3) 10 times, SSM. (80 sts)

Now work in herringbone edging as folls:
Edging round 1: (yarn forward, slip 2 sts, yarn back, K2) 20 times, SSM.
Edging round 2: (K1, yarn forward, slip 2 sts, yarn back, K1) 20 times, SSM.
Edging round 3: (K2, yarn forward, slip 2 sts, yarn back) 20 times, SSM.
Edging round 4: K3, (yarn forward, slip 2 sts, yarn back, K2) 19 times, K1, SSM.
Change to yarn B (held double) and work edging rounds 1 – 4 once more.
Change to yarn C (held double) and work edging rounds 1 – 4 once more.
Edging round 13: (K2, yarn forward, slip 2 sts, yarn back) 20 times, SSM.
Edging round 14: (K1, yarn forward, slip 2 sts, yarn back, K1) 20 times, SSM.
Edging round 15: (yarn forward, slip 2 sts, yarn back, K2) 20 times, SSM.
Edging round 16: K3, (yarn forward, slip 2 sts, yarn back, K2) 19 times, K1, SSM.

Change to yarn B (held double) and work edging rounds 13 – 16 once more.
Change to yarn A (held double) and work edging rounds 13 – 16 once more.

Next round: Knit, SSM.
Next round: Purl, SSM.

Change to yarn B (held double).
Next round: Knit, SSM.
Next round: (K1, P1) to end, SSM.

Change to yarn C (held double).
Next round: (P1, K1) to end, SSM.
Next round: (K1, P1) to end, SSM.
The last 2 rounds form seed stitch.
Work a further 18 rounds in seed stitch.

Change to yarn B (held double) and work 2 rounds in seed stitch.
Change to yarn C (held double) and work 2 rounds in seed stitch.
Change to yarn B (held double) and work 10 rounds in seed stitch.

Change to yarn A (held double) and work 2 rounds in seed stitch.
Change to yarn B (held double) and work 2 rounds in seed stitch.
Change to yarn A (held double) and work 6 rounds in seed stitch.

WORK BASE SHAPING
Next round: Knit, SSM.
Next round: Purl, SSM.
Next round (dec): K5, S2K1P, K24, S2K1P, K10, S2K1P, K24, S2K1P, K5, SSM. (72 sts)
Next round: Purl, SSM.
Next round (dec): K4, S2K1P, K22, S2K1P, K8, S2K1P, K22, S2K1P, K4, SSM. (64 sts)
Next round: Purl, SSM.
Next round (dec): K3, S2K1P, K20, S2K1P, K6, S2K1P, K20, S2K1P, K3, SSM. (56 sts)
Next round: Purl, SSM.
Next round (dec): K2, S2K1P, K18, S2K1P, K4, S2K1P, K18, S2K1P, K2, SSM. (48 sts)
Next round: Purl, SSM.
Next round (dec): K1, S2K1P, K16, S2K1P, K2, S2K1P, K16, S2K1P, K1, SSM. (40 sts)
Next round: Purl, SSM.
Next round (dec): S2K1P, K14, S2K1P, S2K1P, K14, S2K1P, SSM. (32 sts)

Turn purse to WS and starting at marker slip 16 sts onto first side of circular needle, slip remaining 16 sts onto second side of circular needle.
Take a third needle and cast off 16 sts using the 3 needle cast off method.

MAKING UP
Sew in all ends.

SMALL FLOWERS
Make 22 flowers using remnants of yarn.
Using 4.5 mm (US 7) needles and one strand of chosen remnant yarn cast on 26 sts.
Row 1: K1, cast off 4 sts, 2 sts on RH needle, cast off 4 sts, 3 sts on RH needle, cast off 4 sts, 4 sts on RH needle, cast off 4 sts, 5 sts on RH needle, cast off 4 sts, 6 sts on RH needle.
Break yarn, thread through rem sts, draw up and fasten off.
Using photograph as a guide, sew flowers around the base of the edging band of purse.
Sew on purse handles. ❀

PEGGY
PRETTY COLLAR

This pretty collar is a modern interpretation of an historical idea. Today's collars descend from the ruffle created by the drawstring at the neck of the medieval chemise, followed by the highly elaborate Elizabethan ruff. Separate collars have existed since the mid-16th century; during the Edwardian period and sporadically thereafter, ornamental collars have been worn as a form of jewelry.

ONE SIZE
Approx. 39.5 cm (15½ in)
(neck measurement at cast off)

YARN
3
Knitted in Double Knitting–weight yarn
Photographed using 1 x 50g/250m (1.75oz/273yd) ball of Louisa Harding *Amitola* in 107 Tango

NEEDLES
Pair of 4 mm (US 6) knitting needles

TENSION/GAUGE
22 sts x 30 rows to 10 cm (4 in) square measured over st st using 4 mm (US 6) knitting needles.

EXTRAS
2 metres (79 in) of fine ribbon

SPECIAL ABBREVIATION
SSK – slip 2 sts knitwise one at a time from the LH needle to the RH needle,
insert LH needle tip through both front loops and knit together.

Peggy Pretty Collar

Using 4 mm (US 6) needles and using the cable cast on method, work picot cast on as folls:
*Cast on 5 sts using the cable cast on method,
cast off 2 sts, slip st on RH needle back onto LH needle
(3 sts now on LH needle), rep from * 44 times more,
cast on 1 st. (136 sts)

Work 2 rows in garter st.

Now work 24 rows in patt as folls:

Patt row 1: K2, (K5, yo, K4, SSK) 12 times, K2.

Patt row 2, 4, 6, 8, & 10: K2, P132, K2.

Patt row 3: K2, (K2tog, K3, yo, K1, yo, K3, SSK) 12 times, K2.

Patt row 5: K2, (K2tog, K2, yo, K1, yo, SSK, yo, K2, SSK) 12 times, K2.

Patt row 7: K2, (K2tog, K1, yo, K1, [yo, SSK] twice, yo, K1, SSK) 12 times, K2.

Patt row 9: K2, (K2tog, yo, K1, [yo, SSK] 4 times) 12 times, K2.

Patt row 11 (dec): K2, (K2tog, [K1, P1] 3 times, K1, SSK) 12 times, K2. (112 sts)

Patt row 12: K2, (P2, [K1, P1] 3 times, P1) 12 times, K2.

Patt row 13 (dec): K2, (K2tog, [P1, K1] twice, P1, SSK) 12 times, K2. (88 sts)

Patt row 14, 16, & 18: K2, (P1, [K1, P1] 3 times) 12 times, K2.

Patt row 15 & 17: K2, ([K1, P1] 3 times, K1) 12 times, K2.

Patt row 19 (dec): K2, [K1, P1] 3 times, K2tog, (P1, [K1, P1] 2 times, K2tog) 10 times, [P1, K1] 3 times, K2. (77 sts)

Patt row 20: Knit.
Patt row 21: Knit.

Patt row 22 (WS)(eyelets): K2, P1, (yo, P2tog) 36 times, K2.

Patt row 23: Knit.

Patt row 24: Knit.

Cast off taking care not to pull stitches too tightly.

Making up
Sew in all ends.
Press/block collar as described on page 138.
Thread ribbon through eyelet holes.
Secure with a bow.

LULU
Lacy Capelet

I have many family nicknames, Lulu being one of them! My family and I have spent many happy summers escaping from the chill of the English weather, choosing to holiday in the sunny Cote d'Azure. Lulu is my French alter ego. This little capelet is perfect for chilly summer evenings: slip it on as dusk descends. Not only does it snuggle the shoulders, but the addition of sleeves adds to its cosiness.

ONE SIZE
Circumference at hem: 55 cm (61 in)
Circumference at shoulder: 62 cm (24½ in)
Length: 35.5 cm (14 in)

YARN
(4)
Knitted in Aran-weight yarn
Photographed using 6 x 50g/90m (1.75 oz/98yd) balls of Louisa Harding *Akiko* in 010 Girly

NEEDLES
5 mm (US 8) 100cm (40 in) circular knitting needle
4.5 mm (US 7) 80cm (32 in) circular knitting needle (4.5 mm dpns)
Stitch marker

TENSION/GAUGE
18 sts x 24 rows to 10 cm (4 in) square measured over patt using 5 mm (US 8) knitting needles.

SPECIAL ABBREVIATIONS
SSK – slip 2 sts knitwise one at a time from the LH needle to the RH needle,
insert LH needle tip through both front loops and knit together.
RC – right cross, knit next 2 stitches on LH needle together, without removing the stitches from the needle,
knit the first st again, slip both stitches from needle.
SSM – slip stitch marker.

NOTE
When casting on a large number of stitches I find that it helps to put in a stitch marker after
every 20 sts cast on which helps with keeping the stitch count.

Lulu Lacy Capelet

Using 5 mm (US 8) circular needle cast on 280 sts.
Foundation round 1: Knit, place stitch marker.
Foundation round 2: Purl, slip stitch marker - SSM.

Now work 10 rounds in lace and rev st st panels setting sts as folls:
Lace round 1: (K2, K2tog, yo, RC, yo, SSK, K2, P10) 14 times, SSM.
Lace round 2 & 4: (K10, P10) 14 times, SSM.
Lace round 3: (K1, K2tog, yo, K4, yo, SSK, K1, P10) 14 times, SSM.
Lace round 5: (K2tog, yo, K1, K2tog, [yo] twice, SSK, K1, yo, SSK, P10) 14 times, SSM.
Lace round 6: (K4, K into front and back of double yo on previous row, K4, P10) 14 times, SSM.
Lace round 7: (K2, yo, SSK, K2, K2tog, yo, K2, P10) 14 times, SSM.
Lace round 8: (K10, P10) 14 times, SSM.
Lace round 9: (K3, yo, SSK, K2tog, yo, K3, P10) 14 times, SSM.
Lace round 10: (K10, P10) 14 times, SSM.

Work lace rounds 1 – 8 once more.

Lace round 19 (dec): (K3, yo, SSK, K2tog, yo, K3, P2tog, P6, P2tog) 14 times, SSM. (252 sts)
Lace round 20, 22, & 24: (K10, P8) 14 times, SSM.
Lace round 21: (K2, K2tog, yo, RC, yo, SSK, K2, P8) 14 times, SSM.
Lace round 23: (K1, K2tog, yo, K4, yo, SSK, K1, P8) 14 times, SSM.
Lace round 25: (K2tog, yo, K1, K2tog, [yo] twice, SSK, K1, yo, SSK, P8) 14 times, SSM.
Lace round 26: (K4, K into front and back of double yo on previous row, K4, P8) 14 times, SSM.
Lace round 27: (K2, yo, SSK, K2, K2tog, yo, K2, P8) 14 times, SSM.
Lace round 28: (K10, P8) 14 times, SSM.

Lace round 29 (dec): (K3, yo, SSK, K2tog, yo, K3, P2tog, P4, P2tog) 14 times, SSM. (224 sts)
Lace round 30, 32, & 34: (K10, P6) 14 times, SSM.
Lace round 31: (K2, K2tog, yo, RC, yo, SSK, K2, P6) 14 times, SSM.
Lace round 33: (K1, K2tog, yo, K4, yo, SSK, K1, P6) 14 times, SSM.
Lace round 35: (K2tog, yo, K1, K2tog, [yo] twice, SSK, K1, yo, SSK, P6) 14 times, SSM.
Lace round 36: (K4, K into front and back of double yo on previous row, K4, P6) 14 times, SSM.
Lace round 37: (K2, yo, SSK, K2, K2tog, yo, K2, P6) 14 times, SSM.
Lace round 38: (K10, P6) 14 times, SSM.

Lace round 39 (dec): (K3, yo, SSK, K2tog, yo, K3, P2tog, P2, P2tog) 14 times, SSM. (196 sts)
Lace round 40, 42, & 44: (K10, P4) 14 times, SSM.
Lace round 41: (K2, K2tog, yo, RC, yo, SSK, K2, P4) 14 times, SSM.
Lace round 43: (K1, K2tog, yo, K4, yo, SSK, K1, P4) 14 times, SSM.
Lace round 45: (K2tog, yo, K1, K2tog, [yo] twice, SSK, K1, yo, SSK, P4) 14 times, SSM.
Lace round 46: (K4, K into front and back of double yo on previous row, K4, P4) 14 times, SSM.
Lace round 47: (K2, yo, SSK, K2, K2tog, yo, K2, P4) 14 times, SSM.
Lace round 48: (K10, P4) 14 times, SSM.

Lace round 49 (dec): (K3, yo, SSK, K2tog, yo, K3, [P2tog] twice) 14 times, SSM. (168 sts)
Lace round 50, 52, & 54: (K10, P2) 14 times, SSM.
Lace round 51: (K2, K2tog, yo, RC, yo, SSK, K2, P2) 14 times, SSM.
Lace round 53: (K1, K2tog, yo, K4, yo, SSK, K1, P2) 14 times, SSM.
Lace round 55: (K2tog, yo, K1, K2tog, [yo] twice, SSK, K1, yo, SSK, P2) 14 times, SSM.
Lace round 56: (K4, K into front and back of double yo on previous row, K4, P2) 14 times, SSM.
Lace round 57: (K2, yo, SSK, K2, K2tog, yo, K2, P2) 14 times, SSM.
Lace round 58: (K10, P2) 14 times, SSM.

Lace round 59 (dec): Remove the stitch marker, slip the first st, (K2, yo, SSK, K2tog, yo, K2, SSK, K2tog) 13 times, K2, yo, SSK, K2tog, yo, K2, SSK, K2tog (last st of round with first st of last round), slip stitch just worked back onto LH needle, replace marker, (last st worked becomes first st of next round). (140 sts)
Lace round 60, 62, & 64: Knit, SSM.
Lace round 61: (K2, K2tog, yo, RC, yo, SSK, K2) 14 times, SSM.
Lace round 63: (K1, K2tog, yo, K4, yo, SSK, K1) 14 times, SSM.
Lace round 65: (K2tog, yo, K1, K2tog, [yo] twice, SSK, K1, yo, SSK) 14 times, SSM.
Lace round 66: (K4, K into front and back of double yo on previous row, K4) 14 times, SSM.
Lace round 67: (K2, yo, SSK, K2, K2tog, yo, K2) 14 times, SSM.
Lace round 68: Knit, SSM.
Lace round 69: (K3, yo, SSK, K2tog, yo, K3) 14 times, SSM.
Lace round 70: Knit, SSM.
Work lace rounds 61 – 66 once more.

Lulu Lacy Capelet

Lace round 77 (dec): Remove the stitch marker, slip the first st, (K1, yo, SSK, K2, K2tog, yo, K1, K2tog) 13 times, K1, yo, SSK, K2, K2tog, yo, K1, K2tog (last st of round with first st of last round), slip stitch just worked back onto LH needle, replace the stitch marker, (last st worked becomes first st of next round). (126 sts)
Lace round 78: Knit, SSM.
Lace round 79: (K2, yo, SSK, K2tog, yo, K3) 14 times, SSM.
Lace round 80: Knit, SSM.
Lace round 81 (dec): (K3, K2tog, K4) 14 times, SSM. (112 sts)
Lace round 82: Purl, SSM.
Lace round 83: Knit, SSM.
Lace round 84: Turn work and cast off knitwise on the WS, taking care not to pull sts too tightly.

First sleeve

Using photograph as a guide, with RS facing and starting at cast on edge and starting at a rev st st panel, using a 4.5 mm (US 7) circular needle, pick up and K10 sts across cast on edge of rev st st panel, 10 sts from cast on edge of next lace panel, 10 sts from cast on edge of next rev st st panel, 10 sts from cast on edge of next lace panel, 10 sts from cast on edge of next rev st st panel, (50 sts picked up).

Work in rounds with a circular needle or double-pointed needles.
Next round (dec): P15, P2tog, P16, P2tog, P15. (48 sts)

Now work 8 rounds in lace rib setting sts as folls:
Lace rib rounds 1 & 2: (K2, P2) 12 times.
Lace rib round 3: (K2, yo, P2tog) 12 times.
Lace rib rounds 4, 5 & 6: (K2, P2) 12 times.
Lace rib round 7: (K2, P2tog, yo) 12 times.
Lace rib round 8: (K2, P2) 12 times.
These 8 rounds form the lace rib.
Work these 8 rounds twice more.

Next round (dec): (K2, P2tog, K2, P2) 6 times. (42 sts)
Now work in rib setting sts as folls:
Rib round: (K2, P1, K2, P2) 6 times.
This round forms the rib patt, rep this round 9 times.

Next round (dec): (K2, P1, K2, P2tog) 6 times. (36 sts)
Now work in rib setting sts as folls:
Rib round: (K2, P1) 12 times.
This round forms the rib patt, rep this round 9 times.
Cast off in rib.

Second sleeve

With RS facing and cast on edge count 9 panel patts (5 lace panels and 4 rev st st panels) from first sleeve, you should have a rev st st panel next.
Pick up 50 sts as for first sleeve from ** to **.
You should have 9 panel patts between each of the sleeves.

Complete second sleeve as for first sleeve.

Making up

Sew in all ends.
Press/block piece as described on page 138.

Small flowers (make 14)

Using 4.5 mm (US 7) needles cast on 26 sts.
Row 1: K1, cast off 4 sts, 2 sts on RH needle, cast off 4 sts, 3 sts on RH needle, cast off 4 sts, 4 sts on RH needle, Cast off 4 sts, 5 sts on RH needle, cast off 4 sts, 6 sts on RH needle.
Break yarn, thread through rem sts, draw up, fasten off.
Sew flowers into place at the centre of diamonds in lace pattern at top of capelet.

ESTELLE
FERN BOBBLE SCARF

Blood red roses have often been used as darkly gothic inspiration and imagery, and the arched stitch pattern and berry red yarn used for this scarf evoke that feeling in me. The asymmetric lace and bobble pattern mysteriously undulates at the outside edge, creating a naturally occurring gothic flounce which allows the scarf to nestle at the neck effortlessly.

ONE SIZE
Approx. 18 cm (7 in) wide x 81.5 cm (32 in) long

YARN
4
Knitted in Aran-weight yarn
Photographed using 3 x 50g/90m (1.75oz/98yd) balls of Louisa Harding *Akiko* in 014 Berry

NEEDLES
Pair of 6 mm (US 10) knitting needles

TENSION/GAUGE
18 sts x 24 rows to 10 cm (4 in) square measured over bobble and lace patt using 6 mm (US 10) knitting needles.

SPECIAL ABBREVIATIONS
S2KP – slip 2 sts onto RH needle as if going to knit them together, K1,
pass the 2 slipped stitches over the knitted stitch.
SSK – slip 2 sts knitwise one at a time from the LH needle to the RH needle,
insert LH needle tip through both front loops and knit together.
MB – Make bobble, knit into front, back, front, back, front of next st,
(5 sts made) take the first 4 sts over the last st made. (1 stitch)

Estelle Fern Bobble Scarf

Using 6 mm (US 10) needles cast on 35 sts.

Foundation row 1 (RS): Knit.

Foundation row 2: Knit.

Foundation row 3 (dec): K20, S2KP, K12. (33 sts)

Foundation row 4: Knit.

Now work 14 rows in bobble and lace patt setting sts as folls:

Patt row 1 (RS): K5, yo, K2tog, K2, SSK, K6, [yo, K1] twice, S2KP, [K1, yo] twice, K6, K2tog, K1.

Patt row 2: K6, P18, K2, P2, K5.

Patt row 3: K5, yo, K2tog, K2, SSK, K5, yo, K1, yo, K2, S2KP, K2, yo, K1, yo, K5, K2tog, K1.

Patt row 4: K5, P19, K2, P2, K5.

Patt row 5 (inc): K5, yo, K2tog, K2, SSK, K4, yo, K1, yo, MB, P1, K1, S2KP, K1, P1, MB, yo, K1, yo, K7. (34 sts)

Patt row 6: K5, (P5, K1) twice, P8, K2, P2, K5.

Patt row 7 (inc): K5, yo, K2tog, K2, SSK, K3, yo, K1, yo, MB, P1, K2, S2KP, K2, P1, MB, yo, K1, yo, K7. (35 sts)

Patt row 8: K5, P5, (K1, P7) twice, K2, P2, K5.

Patt row 9 (inc): K5, yo, K2tog, K2, SSK, K2, yo, K1, yo, MB, P1, K3, S2KP, K3, P1, MB, yo, K1, yo, K7. (36 sts)

Patt row 10: K5, P5, K1, P9, K1, P6, K2, P2, K5.

Patt row 11 (inc): K5, yo, K2tog, K2, SSK, K1, yo, K1, yo, MB, P1, K4, S2KP, K4, P1, MB, yo, K1, yo, K7. (37 sts)

Patt row 12: K5, P5, K1, P11, K1, P5, K2, P2, K5.

Patt row 13 (inc): K5, yo, K2tog, K2, SSK, yo, K1, yo, MB, P1, K5, S2KP, K5, P1, MB, yo, K1, yo, K7. (38 sts)

Patt row 14 (dec): Cast off 5 sts, (1 st on RH needle) P4, K1, P13, K1, P4, K2, P2, K5. (33 sts)

These 14 rows form the bobble and lace patt.
Work these 14 rows 17 times more, ending with patt row 14.
Work 3 rows in garter st.
Cast off knitwise on WS.

Making up
Sew in all ends.
Press/block scarf as described on page 138. ❧

F A Y E
Ruby Beret

What is it about a beret that evokes images of Parisian mademoiselles? Imagination can lead you to many different inspiration points; this ruby red beret transports me straight into a 1950s photograph. Here we find our English Rose heroine sitting in a café in the winding back streets of Paris, slowly sipping café au lait and reading an intense novel of gothic origin....

ONE SIZE
Approx. 56 cm (22 in) when stretched to fit

YARN
(3)
Knitted in Double Knitting–weight yarn
Photographed using 2 x 50g/110m (1.75oz/120yd) hanks of Louisa Harding *Orielle* in 12 Ruby

NEEDLES
3.5 mm (US 4) 60 cm (24 in) circular needle   4.5 mm (US 7) 60 cm (24 in) circular needle (4.5 mm dpns)
Stitch marker. Crochet hook

TENSION/GAUGE
20 sts x 28 rows to 10 cm (4 in) square measured over st st using 4.5 mm (US 7) circular needle.

SPECIAL ABBREVIATIONS
SSK – slip 2 sts knitwise one at a time from the LH needle to the RH needle,
insert LH needle tip through both front loops and knit together.
RC – right cross – Knit next 2 stitches on LH needle together, without removing the stitches from the needle,
knit the first st again, slip both stitches from needle.
S2KP – slip 2 sts onto RH needle as if going to knit them together, K1,
pass the 2 slipped stitches over the knitted stitch.
SSM – slip stitch marker

NOTE
I find that using a stitch marker placed at the end of each round helps to identify which round is next and where the lace pattern begins and ends. I use the magic loop technique when knitting hats in the round to work the crown shaping decreases. You may find it easier to convert to double-pointed needles.

Faye Ruby Beret

Using 3.5 mm (US 4) circular needle cast on 99 sts.
Foundation round 1: Knit.
Foundation round 2: Purl.

Work in lace rib setting sts as folls:
Rib round 1: (P3, K1, yo, SSK, K2, K2tog, yo, K1) 9 times, place stitch marker.
Rib round 2: (P3, K8) 9 times, SSM.
Rib round 3: (P3, K1, K2tog, yo, RC, yo, SSK, K1) 9 times, SSM.
Rib round 4: (P3, K8) 9 times, SSM.

These 4 rows form the lace rib patt.
Rep these 4 rows 3 times more, ending with RS facing for next row.
Work rib rounds 1 – 3 once more.

Next round (inc): ([P1, M1] twice, P1, K4, yo, K4) 9 times, SSM. (126 sts)
Change to 4.5 mm (US 7) circular needle and work 28 rounds in lace patt setting sts as folls:

Patt round 1 (move stitch marker): ([K2, yo, SSK] twice, K3, K2tog, yo, K1) 9 times, remove stitch marker. K2, replace stitch marker.

Patt round 2, 4, 6, 8, 10, 12 & 14: (K14) 9 times, SSM.

Patt round 3: (K1, yo, SSK, K2, yo, SSK, K1, K2tog, yo, K2, K2tog, yo) 9 times, SSM.
Patt round 5: (K2, yo, SSK, K2, yo, S2KP, yo, K2, K2tog, yo, K1) 9 times, SSM.
Patt round 7: (K3, yo, SSK, K5, K2tog, yo, K2) 9 times, SSM.
Patt round 9: (yo, SSK, K2, yo, SSK, K3, K2tog, yo, K3) 9 times, SSM.
Patt round 11: (K1, yo, SSK, K2, yo, SSK, K1, K2tog, yo, K2, K2tog, yo) 9 times, SSM.
Patt round 13: (K2, yo, SSK, K2, yo, S2KP, yo, K2, K2tog, yo, K1) 9 times, SSM.

Patt round 15: (P1, K2, yo, SSK, K5, K2tog, yo, K2) 9 times, SSM.
Patt round 16: (P1, K13) 9 times, SSM.
Patt round 17: (P2, K2, yo, SSK, K3, K2tog, yo, K2, P1) 9 times, SSM.
Patt round 18: (P2, K11, P1) 9 times, SSM.
Patt round 19: (P3, K2, yo, SSK, K1, K2tog, yo, K2, P2) 9 times, SSM.
Patt round 20: (P3, K9, P2) 9 times, SSM.
Patt round 21: (P4, K2, yo, S2KP, yo, K2, P3) 9 times, SSM.
Patt round 22: (P4, K7, P3) 9 times, SSM.
The last 2 rounds form the lace and rev st st patt.
Work these 2 rounds 3 times more.

SHAPE CROWN
Crown round 1 (dec): (P2tog, P2, K2, yo, S2KP, yo, K2, P1, P2tog) 9 times, SSM. (108 sts)
Crown round 2: (P3, K7, P2) 9 times, SSM.
Crown round 3: (P3, K2, yo, S2KP, yo, K2, P2) 9 times, SSM.
Crown round 4: (P3, K7, P2) 9 times, SSM.
Work the last 2 rounds once more.

Crown round 7 (dec): (P2tog, P1, K2, yo, S2KP, yo, K2, P2tog) 9 times, SSM. (90 sts)
Crown round 8: (P2, K7, P1) 9 times, SSM.
Crown round 9: (P2, K2, yo, S2KP, yo, K2, P1) 9 times, SSM.
Crown round 10: (P2, K7, P1) 9 times, SSM.
Work the last 2 rounds once more.

Crown round 13 (dec)(move stitch marker): P2, (K2, yo, S2KP, yo, K2, P3tog) 8 times, K2, yo, S2KP, yo, K2, slip next st and remove stitch marker, replace st, P3tog, replace stitch marker. (72 sts)
Crown round 14: (K7, P1) 9 times, SSM.
Crown round 15: (K2, yo, S2KP, yo, K2, P1) 9 times, SSM.
Crown round 16: (K7, P1) 9 times, SSM.

Crown round 17 (dec): (SSK, yo, S2KP, yo, K2tog, P1) 9 times, SSM. (54 sts)
Crown round 18: (K5, P1) 9 times, SSM.
Crown round 19: (K1, yo, S2KP, yo, K1, P1) 9 times, SSM.
Crown round 20: (K5, P1) 9 times, SSM.

Crown round 21 (dec): (SSK, K1, K2tog, P1) 9 times, SSM. (36 sts)
Crown round 22: (K3, P1) 9 times, SSM.

Crown round 23 (dec): (S2KP, P1) 9 times, SSM. (18 sts)
Crown round 24: (K1, P1) 9 times, SSM.

Crown round 25 (dec): (SSK) 9 times, SSM. (9 sts)
Crown round 26: Knit, remove stitch marker.
Break yarn, thread through rem sts, draw up and fasten off.

MAKING UP
Sew in all ends.
Press/block beret as described on page 138.
I have used the thread at the top of the beret to make a 5 cm (2 in) single chain with a crochet hook and attached this to the top of the beret. ◉

MYRTLE
FUR COLLAR

Inspired by Jazz Age heroines, this fur yarn collar oozes glamour and theatricality. Quickly knitted,
this simple pattern will enhance your winter wardrobe, turning the humblest coat or jacket into an
eye-catching ensemble guaranteed to turn heads.

ONE SIZE
Approx. measurement at neck 39.5 cm (15½ in)
Approx. measurement at shoulder 59 cm (23 ¼ in)
Length 30.5 cm (12 in)

YARN
Knitted in Super Bulky–weight yarn
Photographed using Louisa Harding *Luzia* and *Grace Silk & Wool*
A. 2 x 50g/40m (1.75oz/43yd) balls of *Luzia* in 007 Otter
B. 1 x 50g/100m (1.75oz/110yd) ball of *Grace Silk & Wool* in 37 Chocolate (yarn used double throughout)

NEEDLES
Pair of 7 mm (US 10½) knitting needles
Pair of 8 mm (US 11) knitting needles

TENSION/GAUGE
11 sts x 14 rows to 10 cm (4 in) square measured over st st using yarn A and 8 mm (US 11) knitting needles.

EXTRAS
2 metres (79 in) of wide satin ribbon

Myrtle Fur Collar

Using 8 mm (US 11) needles and yarn A cast on 65 sts.

Work 2 rows in garter st.

Work 18 rows in st st with garter st edge setting sts as folls:

Row 1: Knit.
Row 2: K2, P61, K2.

Work these 2 rows 8 times more.

Row 19 (RS)(dec): K7, (K2tog, K4) 9 times, K4. (56 sts)

Row 20: K2, P52, K2.

Row 21: Knit.
Row 22: K2, P52, K2.
Work the last 2 rows 3 times more.

Change to 7 mm (US 10½) needles and yarn B (used double throughout) and work eyelet neckband as folls:

Row 29 (RS)(dec): K3, (K2tog, K2) 13 times, K1. (43 sts)
Beg with a K row work 3 rows in garter st, ending with RS facing for next row.

Row 33 (RS)(eyelets): K2, (yo, K2tog) 20 times, K1.
Beg with a K row work 3 rows in garter st, ending with RS facing for next row.

Change to 8 mm (US 11) needles and yarn A.

Row 37 (RS)(inc): K5, (M1, K4) 8 times, M1, K6. (52 sts)

Row 38: K2, P48, K2.

Row 39: Knit.
Row 40: K2, P48, K2.
Work the last 2 rows twice more.

Row 45: Knit.

Beg with a K row work 2 rows in garter st, ending with WS facing for next row.

Cast off knitwise on WS, taking care not to pull stitches too tightly.

Making up
Sew in all ends.
Thread ribbon through eyelets in neckband. ◉

LOLA
CHIC LITTLE PURSE

Knitted in just a few hours, this little purse will add glamour and sophistication to any ensemble. I used the fur yarn *Luzia* in a jewel shade for instant drama; alternatively, knit the purse in a neutral shade, add a leather cross body strap, and turn the project into a casual weekend purse. This very simple pattern can be customised and transformed in many different ways—let your creativity flow.

ONE SIZE
Approx. width at opening 47 cm (18½ in)
Approx. length 24 cm (9½ in)

YARN
Ⓖ
Knitted in Super Bulky–weight yarn
Photographed using Louisa Harding *Grace Silk & Wool* and *Luzia*
A. 1 x 50g/100m (1.75oz/110yd) ball of *Grace Silk & Wool* in 42 Russet (yarn used double throughout)
B. 1 x 50g/40m (1.75oz/43yd) balls of *Luzia* in 002 Ruby

NEEDLES
7 mm (US 10½) 60 cm (24 in)circular knitting needle
8 mm (US 11) 60 cm (24 in) circular knitting needle
Stitch marker

EXTRAS
2 metres (79 in) wide satin ribbon

TENSION/GAUGE
11 sts x 14 rows to 10 cm (4 in) square measured over st st using 8 mm (US 11)
circular knitting needle and yarn B.

NOTE
I find that using a stitch marker placed at the end of each round helps to identify which round
is next and where the eyelet pattern begins and ends.

LOLA CHIC LITTLE PURSE

Using 7 mm (US 10½) circular needle work picot cast on as folls:

Cast on 5 sts using the cable cast on method, cast off 2 sts, slip st on RH needle back onto LH needle (3 sts now on LH needle), rep from * to * 16 times more, cast on 1 st. (52 sts)

Edging round 1: Knit, place stich marker.

Edging round 2: (K1, P1) 26 times, slip stitch marker - SSM.

Edging round 3: (P1, K1) 26 times, SSM.
Work the last 2 rounds once more.

Edging round 6: Knit, SSM.

Edging round 7 (eyelets): (yo, K2tog) 26 times, slip stitch marker - SSM.

Edging round 8: Knit, SSM.

Edging round 9: (K1, P1) 26 times, SSM.

Edging round 10: (P1, K1) 26 times- SSM.
Work the last 2 rounds once more.

Change to 8 mm (US 11) circular needle and yarn B, beg with a K round work in st st until work measures approx. 24 cm (9½ in) from cast on edge or until most of yarn B is used leaving enough yarn to cast off.

Turn purse to WS then divide the stitches evenly between the two ends of the circular needle, 26 sts on each needle. Using a third needle work the 'three needle cast off' to cast off together both sides of the purse.

MAKING UP
Sew in all ends.
Cut ribbon into half. Starting at opposite sides of purse, thread each length of ribbon in and out of eyelet holes around top of purse and knot ends. ✿

CONSTANCE
Rose Bud Mittens

Constance is a girl's name of medieval origin, meaning steadfast and true. These pretty mittens adorned with delicate knitted flowers are simply and quickly knitted. The yarn chosen, with a tiny metallic sliver, enhances the femininity of this project, which although 'girly' will be a steadfast option for keeping the hands warm and toasty throughout the winter months.

ONE SIZE
Width approx. 20 cm (8 in)
(measurement taken before thumb shaping)

YARN
(3)
Knitted in Double Knitting–weight yarn
Photographed using Louisa Harding *Orielle*
A. 1 x 50g/110m (1.75oz/120yd) hank of *Orielle* in 18 Conserve
B. 2 x 50g/110m (1.75oz/120yd) hanks of *Orielle* in 11 Café

NEEDLES
Pair of 3.25 mm (US 3) knitting needles
Pair of 4 mm (US 6) knitting needles

TENSION/GAUGE
22 sts x 30 rows to 10 cm (4 in) square measured over st st using 4 mm (US 6) knitting needles.

NOTE
I have designed these mittens to be knitted flat then seamed.
The experienced knitter can easily convert the mittens to being knitted in the round by decreasing the stitch count by two and not including the selvedge edge stitches.

Constance Rose Bud Mittens

Right hand

Using 4 mm (US 6) needles and yarn A cast on 57 sts and work edging as folls:

Edging row 1 (RS): Knit.
Edging row 2: Knit.
Edging row 3: Knit.
Edging row 4 (eyelets): K1, P1, (yo, P2tog) 27 times, K1.
Edging row 5: Knit.
Edging row 6: Knit.
Edging row 7: Knit.
Edging row 8 (dec): (P1, P2tog) 19 times. (38 sts)

Change to 3.25 mm (US 3) needles and yarn B.
Next row (RS): Knit.
Rib Row 1 (WS): (P2, K2) to last 2 sts, P2.
Rib Row 2 (RS): (K2, P2) to last 2 sts, K2.
These 2 rows form rib.
Work 27 more rows in rib, ending with a WS row. *

Change to 4 mm (US 6) needles and beg with a K row work 8 rows in st st.

Shape thumb

Row 1 (RS): K20, M1, K3, M1, K15. (40 sts)
Work 3 rows.
Row 5: K20, M1, K5, M1, K15. (42 sts)
Work 3 rows.
Cont to inc as above on next row and every foll 4th row to 48 sts.
Work 1 row, ending with a WS row.

Divide for thumb

Next row (RS): K32, turn.
Next row: P13.
Using yarn B and working on these 13 sts only, beg with a K row, work 15 rows in st st.
Next row (WS)(dec): P1, P2tog to end. (7 sts)

Break off yarn, run yarn through rem sts, draw up and fasten off.
Join thumb seam.
With RS facing, rejoin yarn, and using appropriate shade pick up and knit 2 sts from base of thumb and K to end. (37 sts)
Next row: Purl.

**Work 24 rows in st st.

Shape top

Row 1 (RS)(dec): K1, (K2tog tbl, K13, K2tog, K1) twice. (33 sts)
Row 2: Purl.

Row 3 (dec): K1, (K2tog tbl, K11, K2tog, K1) twice. (29 sts)
Row 4: Purl.
Cont to dec on next row and every foll alt row to 21 sts.
Cast off.

Left hand

Work as for Right Hand to *.

Shape thumb

Row 1 (RS): K15, M1, K3, M1, K20. (40 sts)
Work 3 rows.
Row 5: K15, M1, K5, M1, K20. (42 sts)
Work 3 rows.
Cont to inc as above on next row and every foll 4th row to 48 sts.
Work 1 row, ending with a WS row.

Divide for thumb

Next row (RS): K28, turn.
Next row: P13.
Using yarn B and working on these 13 sts only, beg with a K row, work 15 rows in st st.
Next row (WS)(dec): P1, P2tog to end. (7 sts)

Break off yarn, run yarn through rem sts, draw up and fasten off.
Join thumb seam.
With RS facing, rejoin yarn, and using appropriate shade pick up and knit 2 sts from base of thumb and K to end. (37 sts)
Next row: Purl.

Work as for right hand mitten from **.

Small flowers (make 20)

Using 3.25 mm (US 3) needles cast on 26 sts.
Row 1: K1, cast off 4 sts, 2 sts on RH needle, cast off 4 sts, 3 sts on RH needle, cast off 4 sts, 4 sts on RH needle, cast off 4 sts, 5 sts on RH needle, cast off 4 sts, 6 sts on RH needle.
Break yarn, thread through rem sts, draw up and fasten off.

Making up

Sew in ends.
Press/block mittens as described on page 138.
Using photograph as a guide sew 10 flowers around the top of the rib on each of the mittens.
Join side seams together using mattress stitch or back stitch if preferred. 🌹

AGNES
PRINCESS CAPE

This little capelet is designed with a very modern princess in mind. The phrase '*Buon giorno, Principessa*', taken from *Life Is Beautiful*, has become one of my teenage daughter's favourite greetings. We often refer to little girls as 'Princess' as a term of endearment, and to encourage them to believe in themselves, nurture them and fill them with love. I am happy to see that as my daughter grows she embraces the idea that she and her friends are 'Princesses', not with airs and graces, but young, modern and self-assured with confidence to take on life's challenges.

THREE SIZES
Actual size (width at hem): 148 cm (58¼ in), 163 cm (64¼ in), 177 cm (69¾ in)
Finished length: 33cm (13 in), 35 cm (13¾ in), 37.5 cm (14¾ in)

YARN
(6)
Knitted in Super Bulky–weight yarn
Photographed using Louisa Harding *Grace Harmonies* and *Luzia*
A. 2, 3, 3 x 50g/100m (1.75oz/110yd) hanks of *Grace Harmonies* in 07 Beebop (hold yarn double throughout)
B. 3, 5, 6 x 50g/40m (1.75oz/43yd) balls of *Luzia* in 001 Amethyst

NEEDLES
Pair of 7 mm (US 10½) knitting needles
Pair of 8 mm (US 11) knitting needles

EXTRAS
2 metres (79 in) of narrow satin ribbon

TENSION/GAUGE
11 sts x 14 rows to 10 cm (4 in) square measured over st st using 8 mm (US 11) knitting needles and yarn B.

SPECIAL ABBREVIATION
SSM – slip stitch marker.

NOTE
This pattern is knitted from the top down.

AGNES PRINCESS CAPE

Using 7 mm (US 10½) needles and two ends of yarn A work picot cast on as folls:

Cast on 5 sts using the cable cast on method, cast off 2 sts, slip st on RH needle back onto LH needle (3 sts now on LH needle), rep from * 17 times more, cast on 3 sts. (57 sts)

Beg with a K row work 3 rows in garter st, ending with WS facing for next row.

NECKBAND EYELETS
Next row (WS)(eyelets): P1, (yo, P2tog) 28 times.
Next row (RS): Knit.
Next row (WS)(inc): K28, M1, K29. (58 sts)

Change to 8 mm (US 11) needles and work in st st with edging patt and placing markers for raglan shaping as folls:

Next row (RS): Using yarn A - K4, Change to yarn B - K9, place stitch marker, K8, place stitch marker, K16, place stitch marker, K8, place stitch marker, K9, change to yarn A - K4.

Next row (WS): Using yarn A - K4, change to yarn B - P9, slip stitch marker - SSM, P8, SSM, P16, SSM, P8, SSM, P9, Using yarn A - K4.

Raglan row 1 (RS)(inc): Using yarn A – K4, using yarn B – (Knit to 1 st before stitch marker, yo, K1, SSM, K1, yo) 4 times, knit to last 4 sts, using yarn A – K4.

Raglan row 2: Using yarn A K4, using yarn B – Purl to last 4 sts slipping stitch markers, using yarn A – K4.

These raglan rows set the raglan increase pattern. Cont to inc as set on next RS row and every foll RS row until 42(46:50) sts between markers in centre back. 162(178:194) sts.
Work 1 row, ending with RS facing for next row.

Next row (RS): Using yarn A - K4, using yarn B – K to last 4 sts, using yarn A - K4.

Next row: Using yarn A - K4, using yarn B – P to last 4 sts, using yarn A - K4.

Work these 2 rows 3 times more.

Next row (RS): Using yarn A *only* K81(89:97), M1, K81(89:97). (163(179:195) sts.

Work 2 rows in garter st.

Next row (WS)(eyelets): K1, P1, (yo, P2tog) 80(88:96) times, K1.
Work 3 rows in garter st.
Cast off knitwise on WS.

MAKING UP
Sew in ends,
Thread ribbon through eyelets in neckband. ◉

MURIEL
Paisley Capelet

This design takes its inspiration from traditional paisley motif shawls. Originally produced by artisans in Northern India, the 'Kashmir shawl' was an intricate tapestry-woven fine wool shawl. These shawls became a luxury commodity as fashionable wraps for the ladies of the English and French elite by the 1700s. However, as demand grew and the Jacquard loom was invented in Europe, the shawls began to be produced in Paisley, Scotland. The characteristic Kashmiri motif of the mango shape began to be known simply as the paisley.

TWO SIZES
Circumference at hem: 89.5 cm (35¼ in), 107 cm(42 in)
Capelet length: 32 cm (12 ½ in)

YARN

Knitted in Worsted-weight yarn
Photographed using 4, 5 x 50g/100m (1.75oz/110yd) hanks of Louisa Harding *Grace Harmonies* in 04 Melody

NEEDLES
Pair of 4.5 mm (US 7) knitting needles
Cable needle   Stitch marker.

TENSION/GAUGE
20 sts x 28 rows to 10 cm (4 in) square measured over patt using 4.5 mm (US 7) knitting needles.

EXTRAS
7 small mother-of-pearl buttons

SPECIAL ABBREVIATIONS
SSK – slip 2 sts knitwise one at a time from the LH needle to the RH needle,
insert LH needle tip through both front loops and knit together.
SK2togP – slip 1 st, K2tog, pass the slipped stitch over the stitches knitted together.
S2K1P – slip 2 sts together from LH needle to RH needle (as if knitting them together), K1, pass the 2 slipped stitches over the stitch knitted.
C8B – slip 4 sts onto cable needle, hold at back, K4, K4 from cable needle.
M1P – make one stitch purlwise, pick up the horizontal loop before next stitch and purl into the back of it.
SSM – slip stitch marker

MURIEL PAISLEY CAPELET

Using 4.5 mm (US 7) needles work picot cast on as folls:
*Cast on 5 sts using the cable cast on method, cast off
2 sts, slip st on RH needle back onto LH needle*
(2 sts now on LH needle), rep from * 20 times more,
cast on 1 st. (64 sts)

Edging row 1 (RS): Knit.
Edging row 2: Knit.
Edging row 3: Knit.

Edging row 4 (eyelets)(picot): Cast on 2 sts, cast off 2 sts,
(1 st on RH needle) K2, P1, (yo, P2tog) 30 times.

Edging row 5: Knit.
Edging row 6: Knit.

Edging row 7 (inc): K14, M1, K2, M1, K6, place stitch
marker, K42. (66 sts)

Edging row 8 (picot): Cast on 2 sts, cast off 2 sts,
(1 st on RH needle) K2, P37, K2, slip stitch marker - SSM,
P2, K2, P8, K2, P2, K8.

Now work 48 rows in cable and paisley lace patt setting
sts as folls:
Patt row 1: K8, K2tog, yo, K12, yo, SSK, SSM,
K25, (K2tog, yo) twice, K1, yo, SSK, K10.

Patt row 2, 6, 10, 14, 18, 22, 26, 30, 34, 38, 42, & 46:
K3, P37, K2, SSM, P2, K2, P8, K2, P2, K8.

Patt row 3: K8, yo, SSK, K12, K2tog, yo, SSM,
K24, K2tog, yo, K5, yo, SSK, K9.

Patt row 4, 8, 12, 16, 20, 24, 28, 32, 36, 40, & 44 (picot):
Cast on 2 sts, cast off 2 sts, (1 st on RH needle) K2, P37,
K2, SSM, P2, K2, P8, K2, P2, K8.

Patt row 5: K8, K2tog, yo, K12, yo, SSK, SSM,
K23, K2tog, yo, K7, yo, SSK, K8.

Patt row 7 (cable): K8, yo, SSK, K2, C8B, K2, K2tog, yo, SSM,
K22, K2tog, yo, K3, yo, SK2togP, yo, K3, yo, SSK, K7.

Patt row 9: K8, K2tog, yo, K12, yo, SSK, SSM,
K22, K2tog, yo, K4, yo, SK2togP, yo, K3, yo, SSK, K6.

Patt row 11: K8, yo, SSK, K12, K2tog, yo, SSM,
K22, K2tog, yo, K5, yo, SK2togP, yo, K2, yo, SK2togP, yo, K5.

Patt row 13: K8, K2tog, yo, K12, yo, SSK, SSM,
K23, yo, SSK, K4, yo, S2K1P, yo, K2, yo, S2K1P, yo, K5.

Patt row 15: K8, yo, SSK, K12, K2tog, yo, SSM,
K9, K2tog, yo, K1, (yo, SSK) twice, K8, yo, SSK, K3, yo,
K3tog, yo, K2, yo, S2K1P, yo, K5.

Patt row 17: K8, K2tog, yo, K12, yo, SSK, SSM,
K8, K2tog, yo, K5, yo, SSK, K8, yo, SSK, K2, K2tog, yo, K3,
yo, K3tog, yo, K5.

Patt row 19 (cable): K8, yo, SSK, K2, C8B, K2, K2tog, yo, SSM,
K7, K2tog, yo, K7, yo, SSK, K8, yo, SSK, K5, yo, K3tog,
yo, K6.

Patt row 21: K8, K2tog, yo, K12, yo, SSK, SSM,
K6, K2tog, yo, K3, yo, K3tog, yo, K3, yo, SSK, K8, yo, SSK,
K4, K2tog, yo, K7.

Patt row 23: K8, yo, SSK, K12, K2tog, yo, SSM,
K5, K2tog, yo, K3, yo, K3tog, yo, K4, yo, SSK, K9, yo, SSK,
K2, K2tog, yo, K8.

Patt row 25: K8, K2tog, yo, K12, yo, SSK, SSM,
K4, yo, K3tog, yo, K2, yo, K3tog, yo, K5, yo, SSK, K10,
yo, SSK, K2tog, yo, K9.

Patt row 27: K8, yo, SSK, K12, K2tog, yo, SSM,
K4, yo, S2K1P, yo, K2, yo, S2K1P, yo, K4, K2tog, yo, K5,
yo, K3tog, yo, K3, yo, K3tog, yo, K10.

Patt row 29: K8, K2tog, yo, K12, yo, SSK, SSM,
K4, yo, S2K1P, yo, K2, yo, SK2togP, yo, K3, K2tog, yo, K5,
yo, K3tog, yo, K3, yo, K3tog, yo, K11.

Patt row 31 (cable): K8, yo, SSK, K2, C8B, K2, K2tog, yo, SSM,
K4, yo, SK2togP, yo, K3, yo, SSK, K2, K2tog, yo, K7, yo,
SK2togP, yo, K1, yo, K3tog, yo, K12.

Patt row 33: K8, K2tog, yo, K12, yo, SSK, SSM,
K5, yo, SK2togP, yo, K5, K2tog, yo, K9, yo, SSK, yo, K3tog,
yo, K13.

Patt row 35: K8, yo, SSK, K12, K2tog, yo, SSM,
K6, yo, SSK, K4, K2tog, yo, K28.

Patt row 37: K8, K2tog, yo, K12, yo, SSK, SSM,
K7, yo, SSK, K2, K2tog, yo, K29.

Patt row 39: K8, yo, SSK, K12, K2tog, yo, SSM,
K8, yo, SSK, K2tog, yo, K30.

Patt row 41: K8, K2tog, yo, K12, yo, SSK, SSM, K9,
yo, SK2togP, yo, K3, yo, SK2togP, yo, K24.

Muriel Paisley Capelet

Patt row 43 (cable): K8, yo, SSK, K2, C8B, K2, K2tog, yo, SSM, K10, yo, SK2togP, yo, K3, yo, SK2togP, yo, K23.

Patt row 45: K8, K2tog, yo, K12, yo, SSK, SSM, K11, yo, SK2togP, yo, K1, yo, K3tog, yo, K24.

Patt row 47: K8, yo, SSK, K12, K2tog, yo, SSM, K12, yo, SK2togP, yo, K2tog, yo, K25.

Patt row 48 (picot): Cast on 2 sts, cast off 2 sts, (1 st on RH needle) K2, P37, K2, P2, K2, P8, K2, SSM, P2, K8.
These 48 rows for the cable and paisley lace patt.

Work these 48 rows 4(5) times more, ending with patt row 48 and RS facing for next row.

Now work 7 rows in edging patt as folls:
Edging row 1 (dec): K13, SSK, K2, K2tog, K5, remove stitch marker, K42. (64 sts)
Edging row 2: Knit.
Edging row 3: Knit.

Edging row 4 (eyelets)(picot): Cast on 2 sts, cast off 2 sts, (1 st on RH needle) K2, P1, (yo, P2tog) 30 times.

Edging row 5: Knit.
Edging row 6: Knit.
Edging row 7: Knit.

Cast off on the WS using the picot cast off method as folls:
With first st on LH needle, *cast on 2 sts, then cast off 5 sts, rep from * 20 times.

Making up
Sew in all ends.
Press/block piece as described on page 138.
Sew on 7 buttons to yoke section of capelet using photograph as a guide.
Use eyelet band on opposite side as buttonholes. ✿

EVELYN
GLAMOROUS BOBBLE HATS

Sometimes when you're designing it's fun to play with contradictory ideas. The practical ideal of the bobble hat is to keep you wrapped up and warm in winter. In this project I wanted to play with this concept, turning the humble bobble hat into something far more glamorous, selecting a silk and wool self-beading yarn to make it glisten and twinkle.

ONE SIZE
Approx. 56 cm (22 in) when stretched to fit

YARN
(4)
Knitted in Aran-weight yarn
Striped tonal hat: Photographed using Louisa Harding *Grace Hand Beaded* and *Grace Harmonies*
A. 1 x 50g/67.5m (1.75oz/74) hank of *Grace Hand Beaded* in 17 Festive
B. 2 x 50g/100m (1.75 oz/110yd) hanks of *Grace Harmonies* in 06 Swing
One-colour hat: Photographed using 2 x 50g/90m (1.75 oz/98yd) balls of Louisa Harding *Akiko* in 008 Bluster

NEEDLES
4.5 mm (US 7) 60 cm (24 in) circular knitting needle   5 mm (US 8) 60 cm (24 in) circular knitting needle (5 mm dpns)
Cable needle

TENSION/GAUGE
18 sts x 24 rows to 10 cm (4 in) square measured over st st using 5 mm (US 8) knitting needles.

SPECIAL ABBREVIATIONS
MB – make bobble, knit into the front and back of the next st twice and then into the front once more,
(5 sts made), take the first 4 sts made over the last st made (1 st).
SSK – slip 2 sts knitwise one at a time from the LH needle to the RH needle,
insert LH needle tip through both front loops and knit together.
C6F – slip 3 sts onto cable needle, hold at front, K3, K3 from cable needle.
M1 – make 1 stitch by picking up the horizontal loop before next stitch, work into the back of it knitwise.
SSM – slip stitch marker.

NOTE
I find that using a stitch marker placed at the end of each round helps to identify which round is next and where the cable pattern begins and ends. I use the magic loop technique when knitting hats in the round.

Evelyn Glamorous Bobble Hats

Striped tonal hat

Using a 4.5 mm (US 7) circular needle and yarn A work bobble cast on as folls:
Using the cable cast on method cast on 3 sts, make a bobble into the 3rd stitch cast on (MB – make bobble, knit into the front and back of the 3rd cast on st twice, then into the front once more, [5 sts made], take the first 4 sts made over the last st made [1 st]), 3 sts on needle, *cast on 5 sts, make a bobble into the last st cast on, rep from * 17 times, cast on 2 sts, place stitch marker. (90 sts)

Work 18 rounds in striped rib setting sts as folls:

Rib round 1: (P1, K3, P1) 18 times, SSM.
Rib round 2: (P1, K3, P1) 18 times, SSM.
Change to yarn B and work 4 rounds in rib.

These 6 rounds form the striped rib.
Work these 6 rounds twice more.

Cont to work in 6 round stripe repeat, 2 rounds A, 4 rounds B and work patt as folls:

Next round: (P1, M1, K2, SSK, K2tog, K2, M1, P1) 9 times, SSM.
Next round (inc): (P2, K6, P2, M1) 9 times, SSM. (99 sts)

Next round: (P2, K6, P2, K1) 9 times, SSM.
Work the last round 9 times more.

Change to 5 mm (US 8) circular needle and work 12 rounds in striped cable and bobble patt as folls:

Cable round 1: (P2, C6F, P2, MB) 9 times, SSM.
Cable round 2, 3 & 4: (P2, K6, P2, K1) 9 times, SSM.
Cable round 5: (P2, K6, P2, MB) 9 times, SSM.
Cable round 6, 7 & 8: (P2, K6, P2, K1) 9 times, SSM.
Cable round 9: (P2, K6, P2, MB) 9 times, SSM.
Cable round 10, 11 & 12: (P2, K6, P2, K1) 9 times, SSM.

Work cable rounds 1 - 8 once more.

Cable round 21 (dec): (P2tog, K6, P2tog, MB) 9 times, SSM. (81 sts)
Cable round 22, 23 & 24: (P1, K6, P1, K1) 9 times, SSM.
Cable round 25: (P1, C6F, P1, MB) 9 times, SSM.
Cable round 26: (P1, K6, P1, K1) 9 times, SSM.

Cable round 27 (dec): (P1, K1, SSK, K2tog, K1, P1, K1) 9 times, SSM. (63 sts)
Cable round 28: (P1, K4, P1, K1) 9 times, SSM.
Cable round 29: (P1, K4, P1, MB) 9 times, SSM.
Cable round 30: (P1, K4, P1, K1) 9 times, SSM.

Cable round 31 (dec): (P1, K1, K2tog, K1, P1, K1) 9 times, SSM. (54 sts)
Cable round 32: (P1, K3, P1, K1) 9 times, SSM.
Cable round 33: (P1, K3, P1, MB) 9 times, SSM.
Cable round 34: (P1, K3, P1, K1) 9 times, SSM.

Cable round 35 (dec): (P1, Sl1, K2tog, psso, P1, K1) 9 times, SSM. (36 sts)
Cable round 36: (P1, K1) 18 times, SSM.

Cable round 37 (dec): (K2tog) 18 times, SSM. (18 sts)
Cable round 38: Knit, SSM.

Cable round 39 (dec): (K2tog) 9 times, remove stitch marker. (9 sts)

Break yarn, thread through rem sts, draw up and fasten off.

Making up

Sew in all ends.
Using yarn B make a 5 cm (2 in) pompom.
Attach to the top of hat by securing pompom with a few stitches inside the hat.

One-colour hat

Work as for striped tonal hat, working in one colour throughout. 🌀

LAVERNE
Beautiful Bloom Scarves

Both variations of this scarf are adorned with knitted blooms, and both involve embellishments which use time-consuming techniques. The hand-finishing process reminds me of the seamstresses working in artisan ateliers in Paris for the 'haute couture' fashion houses. These lavishly decorated scarves will showcase not only creative individuality but the great skill required to produce them.

SIZE
Flower garland scarf: Approx. 17 cm (6¾ in) wide x 130 cm (51 in) long
Rosette scarf: Approx. 15 cm (6 in) wide x 109 cm (43 in) long

YARN
(4)
Flower garland scarf: Knitted in Worsted-weight yarn
Photographed using 3 x 50g/100m (1.75oz/110yd) hanks of Louisa Harding *Grace Harmonies* in 07 Bebop
(3)
Rosette scarf: Knitted in Double Knitting–weight yarn
Photographed using 1 x 50g/250m (1.75oz/273yd) ball of Louisa Harding *Amitola* in 112 Dijon

EXTRAS
Flower garland scarf: 83 flowers knitted in Louisa Harding *Grace Silk & Wool*
1 x 50g/100m (1.75oz/110yd) ball each of 40 Festive; 41 India; 42 Russet
Rosette scarf: Button and brooch back for rosette

NEEDLES
Flower garland scarf: Pair of 5 mm (US 8) knitting needles   Pair of 3.75 mm (US 5) knitting needles (for flowers)
Rosette scarf: Pair of 4.5 mm (US 7) knitting needles (for rosette)

TENSION/GAUGE
Flower garland scarf: 18 sts x 24 rows to 10 cm (4 in) square measured over lace patt using 5 mm (US 8) knitting needles.
Rosette scarf: 23 sts x 28 rows to 10 cm (4 in) square measured over lace patt using 4.5 mm (US 7) knitting needles.

SPECIAL ABBREVIATIONS
S2KP – slip 2 sts onto RH needle as if going to knit them together, K1, pass the 2 slipped stitches over the knitted stitch.
SSK – slip 2 sts knitwise one at a time from the LH needle to the RH needle,
insert LH needle tip through both front loops and knit together.

Laverne Beautiful Bloom Scarves

Flower garland scarf

Using 5 mm (US 8) needles cast on 35 sts.
*Work 10 rows in edging patt setting sts as folls:
Edging row 1 (RS): Knit.
Edging row 2: Knit.
Edging row 3: K3, yo, SSK, K25, K2tog, yo, K3.
Edging row 4: K3, P2, K25, P2, K3.
Edging row 5: K3, yo, SSK, K6, yo, S2KP, yo, K7, yo, S2KP, yo, K6, K2tog, yo, K3.
Edging row 6: K3, P2, K6, P3, K7, P3, K6, P2, K3.
Edging row 7: K3, yo, SSK, K4, (K2tog, yo, K3, yo, SSK, K3) twice, K1, K2tog, yo, K3.
Edging row 8: K3, P2, (K5, P5) twice, K5, P2, K3.
Edging row 9: K3, yo, SSK, K3, (K2tog, yo, K5, yo, SSK, K1) twice, K2, K2tog, yo, K3.
Edging row 10: K3, P2, K4, (P7, K3) twice, K1, P2, K3.

Now work 12 rows in lace and edging patt setting sts as folls:

Patt row 1: K3, yo, SSK, K2, K2tog, yo, K7, yo, S2KP, yo, K7, yo, SSK, K2, K2tog, yo, K3.
Patt row 2, 4, 6, 8, 10 & 12: K3, P2, K2, P21, K2, P2, K3.
Patt row 3: K3, yo, SSK, K4, (yo, SSK, K3, K2tog, yo, K3) twice, K1, K2tog, yo, K3.
Patt row 5: K3, yo, SSK, K5, (yo, SSK, K1, K2tog, yo, K5) twice, K2tog, yo, K3.
Patt row 7: K3, yo, SSK, K6, yo, S2KP, yo, K7, yo, S2KP, yo, K6, K2tog, yo, K3
Patt row 9: K3, yo, SSK, K4, (K2tog, yo, K3, yo, SSK, K3) twice, K1, K2tog, yo, K3.
Patt row 11: K3, yo, SSK, K3, (K2tog, yo, K5, yo, SSK, K1) twice, K2, K2tog, yo, K3.
These 12 rows form the lace pattern.*
Work these 12 rows 26 times more, ending with patt row 12.

**Work 11 rows in edging patt as folls:
Edging row 1 (RS): K3, yo, SSK, K2, K2tog, yo, K7, yo, S2KP, yo, K7, yo, SSK, K2, K2tog, yo, K3.
Edging row 2: K3, P2, K4, (P7, K3) twice, K1, P2, K3.
Edging row 3: K3, yo, SSK, K4, (yo, SSK, K3, K2tog, yo, K3) twice, K1, K2tog, yo, K3.
Edging row 4: K3, P2, (K5, P5) twice, K5, P2, K3.
Edging row 5: K3, yo, SSK, K5, (yo, SSK, K1, K2tog, yo, K5) twice, K2tog, yo, K3.
Edging row 6: K3, P2, K6, P3, K7, P3, K6, P2, K3.
Edging row 7: K3, yo, SSK, K6, yo, S2KP, yo, K7, yo, S2KP, yo, K6, K2tog, yo, K3
Edging row 8: K3, P2, K25, P2, K3.
Edging row 9: K3, yo, SSK, K25, K2tog, yo, K3.
Edging row 10: Knit.
Edging row 11: Knit.
Cast off knitwise on WS.

Making up
Sew in all ends, press/block as on page 138.

Small flowers
Using 3.75 mm (US 5) needles cast on 26 sts.
Row 1: K1, cast off 4 sts, 2 sts on RH needle, cast off 4 sts, 3 sts on RH needle, cast off 4 sts, 4 sts on RH needle, cast off 4 sts, 5 sts on RH needle, cast off 4 sts, 6 sts on RH needle.
Break yarn, thread through rem sts, draw up, fasten off.
Sew flowers into place at the centre of diamonds in lace pattern.

Rosette scarf
Note - The rosette is made first, the scarf is then made from the remainder of one ball of yarn.

Rosette
Using 4.5 mm (US 7) circular needle cast on 222 sts.
Row 1: Knit.
Row 2: K2, (K1, slip this st back onto LH needle, lift the next 8 sts on LH needle over this st and off needle, knit the first st again, K2) 20 times. (62 sts)
Using short rows work shaping as folls:
Row 3: K54, wrap next st, turn work.
Row 4: Knit.
Row 5: K46, wrap next st, turn work.
Row 6: Knit.
Row 7: K38, wrap next st, turn work.
Row 8: Knit.
Row 9: K30, wrap next st, turn work.
Row 10: Knit.
Row 11: K22, wrap next st, turn work.
Row 12: Knit.
Row 13: K14, wrap next st, turn work.
Row 14: Knit.
Cut yarn and thread through sts on needle, pull tightly to create a rosette, secure with a few stitches and add a button to the rosette centre. Stitch brooch back to reverse of rosette.

Scarf
Using 4.5 mm (US 7) needles cast on 35 sts.
Work as for Flower garland scarf from * to *.
Work these 12 rows 24 times more, ending with patt row 12.
Work 11 rows in edging patt as for flower garland scarf from **.

Making up
Sew in all ends.
Press/block scarf as described on page 138. ❀

IRMA
FLIRTY HAT

Often it is the simplest items that are the most chic. Finished in just a couple of hours, this vintage-inspired hat has all the attributes to make it a flirty, girly and fun project to knit and wear. It's so easy and quick you may need to knit one to coordinate with every ensemble.

ONE SIZE
Approx. 56 cm (22 in) when stretched to fit

YARN
Knitted in Super Bulky–weight yarn
Photographed using Louisa Harding *Luzia* and *Grace Harmonies*
A. 1 x 50g/100m (1.75oz/110yd) hank of *Grace Harmonies* in 08 Rhythm (hold yarn double throughout)
B. 1 x 50g/40m (1.75oz/43yd) ball of *Luzia* in 006 Mink

NEEDLES
7 mm (US 10½) 60 cm (24 in) circular knitting needle (7 mm dpns)
Stitch marker

TENSION/GAUGE
12 sts x 14 rows to 10 cm (4 in) square measured over st st using 7 mm (US 10½)
circular knitting needle and yarn B.

SPECIAL ABBREVIATION
SSM – slip stitch marker.

NOTE
I find that using a stitch marker placed at the end of each round helps to identify which round is next and where the eyelet pattern begins and ends. I use the magic loop technique when knitting hats in the round to work the crown shaping decreases. You may find it easier to convert to double-pointed needles.

Irma Flirty Hat

Using 7 mm (US 10½) circular needle and yarn A used double cast on 54 sts.

Rib round 1: (K3, P3) 9 times, place stitch marker.

Rib round 2: (K3, P3) 9 times, slip stitch marker - SSM.
The last round forms the rib pattern.
Work a further 10 rounds in rib.

Next round (inc): (K3, M1, P3) 9 times, SSM. (63 sts)
Change to yarn B and beg with a K row work 12 rounds in st st.
Now work crown decreases as folls:

Crown round 1 (dec): (K5, K2tog) 9 times, SSM. (54 sts)
Crown round 2, 3 & 4: Knit, SSM.

Crown round 5 (dec): (K4, K2tog) 9 times, SSM. (45 sts)
Crown round 6: Knit, SSM.

Crown round 7 (dec): (K3, K2tog) 9 times, SSM. (36 sts)
Crown round 8: Knit, SSM.

Crown round 9 (dec): (K2, K2tog) 9 times, SSM. (27 sts)
Crown round 10: Knit, SSM.

Crown round 11 (dec): (K1, K2tog) 9 times, SSM. (18 sts)
Crown round 12: Knit, SSM.

Crown round 13 (dec): (K2tog) 9 times, SSM. (9 sts)
Crown round 14: Knit, SSM.
Break yarn, thread through rem sts, draw up and fasten off.

Making up
Sew in all ends.
Using yarn B make a 5 cm (2 in) pompom.
Attach to the top of hat by securing pompom with a few stitches inside the hat. ❀

WINNIE
FLIRTY BOBBLE HATS

Fashion is a fickle thing! Once upon a time, the humble bobble hat was consigned to the winter months only, often knitted by an elderly relative out of oddments of yarn and worn only when absolutely necessary. Today, worn all year round, the bobble hat has its own fashion icon status.
I love a flirty bobble hat: it's practical and fun.

ONE SIZE
Approx. size: 56 cm (22 in) when stretched to fit

YARN
(4)
Knitted in Aran-weight yarn
Photographed in Louisa Harding *Akiko*
Contrast Brim Hat: 1 x 50g/90m (1.75oz/98 yd) ball each of *Akiko* in **A.** 010 Girly **B.** 016 Lavender
Beanie: 2 x 50g/90m (1.75oz/98yd) balls of *Akiko* in 013 Currant

NEEDLES
5 mm (US 8) 60 cm (24 in) circular knitting needle (5 mm dpns)

TENSION/GAUGE
18 sts x 24 rows to 10 cm (4 in) square measured over st st using 5 mm (US 8) knitting needles.

SPECIAL ABBREVIATION
SSM – slip stitch marker.

NOTE
I find that using a stitch marker placed at the end of each round helps to identify which round is next and where the eyelet pattern begins and ends. I use the magic loop technique when knitting hats in the round to work the crown shaping decreases. You may find it easier to convert to double-pointed needles.

Winnie Flirty Bobble Hats

Contrast brim hat

Using a 5 mm (US 8) circular needle and yarn A cast on 90 sts.
*Foundation round 1: Knit.
Foundation round 2: Purl.
Foundation round 3 (eyelets): (yo, K2tog) 45 times.
Foundation round 4: Purl.

Now work 8 rounds in lace patt setting sts as folls:
Lace round 1: (K3, K2tog, K3, yo, P2, yo, K3, SSK, K3) 5 times, place stitch marker.
Lace round 2, 4 & 6: (K8, P2, K8) 5 times, SSM - slip stitch marker.
Lace round 3: (K2, K2tog, K3, yo, K1, P2, K1, yo, K3, SSK, K2) 5 times, SSM.
Lace round 5: (K1, K2tog, K3, yo, K2, P2, K2, yo, K3, SSK, K1) 5 times, SSM.
Lace round 7: (K2tog, K3, yo, K3, P2, K3, yo, K3, SSK) 5 times, SSM.
Lace round 8: (K8, P2, K8) 5 times, SSM.
These 8 rounds form the lace edging patt.*
Work these 8 rounds once more.

Now work in patt setting sts as folls;
Patt round 1: (K4, P2, [K2, P2] twice, K4) 5 times.
This round forms the patt.
Work a further 7 rounds in patt, ending with RS facing for next row.

Now work in rib setting sts as folls;
Rib round 1: (P2, [K2, P2] 4 times) 5 times.
This round forms the rib patt.
Work a further 3 rounds in rib, ending with RS facing for next row.

Change to yarn B and cont to work in rib patt until work measures 20.5 cm (8 in) from cast on edge.

Now work crown decs as folls:
Round 1 (dec): (P2, K2, P2, K2tog, P2, K2tog, P2, K2, P2) 5 times, SSM. (80 sts)
Round 2: (P2, K2, P2, K1, P2, K1, P2, K2, P2) 5 times, SSM.
Round 3 (dec): (P2, K2, P2tog, K1, P2, K1, P2tog tbl, K2, P2) 5 times, SSM. (70 sts)
Round 4: (P2, K2, P1, K1, P2, K1, P1, K2, P2) 5 times, SSM.
Round 5 (dec): (P2, K2tog, P1, K1, P2, K1, P1, K2tog, P2) 5 times, SSM. (60 sts)
Round 6: (P2, K1, P1, K1, P2, K1, P1, K1, P2) 5 times, SSM.
Round 7 (dec): (P2tog tbl, K1, P1, K1, P2, K1, P1, K1, P2tog) 5 times, SSM. (50 sts)
Round 8: ([P1, K1] twice, P2, [K1, P1] twice) 5 times, SSM.
Round 9 (dec): (P1, K1, P1, P2tog tbl, P2tog, P1, K1, P1) 5 times, SSM. (40 sts)
Round 10: (P1, K1, P4, K1, P1) 5 times, SSM.
Round 11 (dec): (P1, P2tog tbl, P2, P2tog, P1) 5 times, SSM. (30 sts)
Round 12: Purl, SSM.
Round 13 (dec): (P2tog tbl, P2, P2tog) 5 times, SSM. (20 sts)
Round 14: Purl, SSM.
Round 15 (dec): (P2tog) 10 times, SSM. (10 sts)
Round 16: Purl, remove stitch marker.
Break yarn, thread through rem sts, draw up, fasten off.

Making up

Sew in all ends. Using yarn B make a 5 cm (2 in) pompom and attach to the top of hat by securing pompom with a few stitches inside the hat.

Beanie

Using a 5 mm (US 8) circular needle cast on 90 sts.
Work as for contrast brim hat from * to *.

Work these 8 rounds three times more.

Now work crown decs as folls:
Round 1 (dec): (K6, K2tog, P2, SSK, K6) 5 times, SSM. (80 sts)
Round 2: (K7, P2, K7) 5 times, SSM.
Round 3 (dec): (K5, K2tog, P2, SSK, K5) 5 times, SSM. (70 sts)
Round 4: (K6, P2, K6) 5 times, SSM.
Round 5 (dec): (K4, K2tog, P2, SSK, K4) 5 times, SSM. (60 sts)
Round 6: (K5, P2, K5) 5 times, SSM.
Round 7 (dec): (K3, K2tog, P2, SSK, K3) 5 times, SSM. (50 sts)
Round 8: (K4, P2, K4) 5 times, SSM.
Round 9 (dec): (K2, K2tog, P2, SSK, K2) 5 times, SSM. (40 sts)
Round 10: (K3, P2, K3) 5 times, SSM.
Round 11 (dec): (K1, K2tog, P2, SSK, K1) 5 times, SSM. (30 sts)
Round 12: (K2, P2, K2) 5 times, SSM.
Round 13 (dec): (K2tog, P2, SSK) 5 times, SSM. (20 sts)
Round 14: (K1, P2, K1) 5 times, remove stitch marker.
Round 15 (dec): slip 1 st, (P2tog, K2tog) 5 times. (10 sts)
Round 16: (P1, K1) 5 times.
Break yarn, thread through rem sts, draw up, fasten off.

Making up

Sew in all ends. Make a 5 cm (2 in) pompom and attach to the top of hat by securing pompom with a few stitches inside the hat. ◉

EUNICE
CORONET CAPELET

I often like to turn knitting upside down, and this design is the outcome of that habit. Knitted from the top down, this pretty capelet uses the naturally occurring points at the cast-on edge to shape and accentuate the neckline. I have chosen a silk and wool blend yarn with fabulous draping properties and an easy lace pattern which neighbours increasing reverse stocking stitch panels to create flirty fullness at the hem.

THREE SIZES
Circumference at shoulder: 64 cm (25¼ in), 72 cm (28¼ in), 80 cm (31½ in)
Circumference at hem: 120 cm (47¼ in), 135 cm (53¼ in), 150 cm (59 in)
Finished length: 30.5 cm (12 in)

YARN
(4)
Knitted in Worsted-weight yarn
Photographed using 4, 6, 8 x 50g/100m (1.75oz/110 yd) hanks of Louisa Harding *Grace Harmonies* in 05 Dizzy

NEEDLES
3.75 mm (US 5) 80cm (32 in) circular knitting needle
4.5 mm (US 7) 80cm (32 in) circular knitting needle
Stitch marker

TENSION/GAUGE
20 sts x 28 rows to 10 cm (4 in) square measured over patt using 4.5 mm (US 7) knitting needles.

SPECIAL ABBREVIATIONS
SSK – slip 2 sts knitwise one at a time from the LH needle to the RH needle,
insert LH needle tip through both front loops and knit together.
S2K1P – slip 2 sts together from LH needle to RH needle (as if knitting them together),
K1, pass the 2 slipped stitches over the stitch knitted.
M1P – make one stitch purlwise, pick up the horizontal loop before next stitch and purl into the back of it.
SSM – slip stitch marker.

NOTE
This project is knitted from the top down. I find that using a stitch marker placed at the end of each round helps to identify which round is next and where the eyelet pattern begins and ends.

Eunice Coronet Capelet

Using 3.75 mm (US 5) circular needle cast on 144 (162:180) sts.

Foundation round 1: Knit.

Foundation round 2: Purl.

Foundation round 3: (yo, K2tog) 72(81:90) times.

Foundation round 4: Purl.

Foundation round 5 (dec): (K9, S2K1P, K6) 8(9:10) times, place stitch marker. (128(144:160) sts)

Foundation round 6: Knit, slip stitch marker - SSM.

Change to 4.5 mm (US 7) circular needle and work 8 rounds in lace and rev st st panels setting sts as folls:

Lace round 1: (K1, P1, K1, yo, K2tog, yo, K3, S2K1P, K3, yo, SSK, yo) 8(9:10) times, SSM.

Lace round 2, 4, 6, & 8: (K1, P1, K14) 8(9:10) times, SSM.

Lace round 3: (K1, P1, K1, yo, K2tog, K1, yo, K2, S2K1P, K2, yo, K1, SSK, yo) 8(9:10) times, SSM.

Lace round 5: (K1, P1, K1, yo, K2tog, K2, yo, K1, S2K1P, K1, yo, K2, SSK, yo) 8(9:10) times, SSM.

Lace round 7: (K1, P1, K1, yo, K2tog, K3, yo, S2K1P, yo, K3, SSK, yo) 8(9:10) times, SSM.

Work lace rounds 1 – 8 once more.

Lace round 17 (inc): (K1, M1P, P1, M1P, K1, yo, K2tog, yo, K3, S2K1P, K3, yo, SSK, yo) 8(9:10) times, SSM. (144(162:180) sts)

Lace round 18, 20, 22, & 24: (K1, P3, K14) 8(9:10) times, SSM.

Lace round 19: (K1, P3, K1, yo, K2tog, K1, yo, K2, S2K1P, K2, yo, K1, SSK, yo) 8(9:10) times, SSM.

Lace round 21: (K1, P3, K1, yo, K2tog, K2, yo, K1, S2K1P, K1, yo, K2, SSK, yo) 8(9:10) times, SSM.

Lace round 23: (K1, P3, K1, yo, K2tog, K3, yo, S2K1P, yo, K3, SSK, yo) 8(9:10) times, SSM.

Lace round 25 (inc): (K1, M1P, P3, M1P, K1, yo, K2tog, yo, K3, S2K1P, K3, yo, SSK, yo) 8(9:10) times, SSM. (160(180:200) sts)

Lace round 26, 28, 30, & 32: (K1, P5, K14) 8(9:10) times, SSM.

Lace round 27: (K1, P5, K1, yo, K2tog, K1, yo, K2, S2K1P, K2, yo, K1, SSK, yo) 8(9:10) times, SSM.

Lace round 29: (K1, P5, K1, yo, K2tog, K2, yo, K1, S2K1P, K1, yo, K2, SSK, yo) 8(9:10) times, SSM.

Lace round 31: (K1, P5, K1, yo, K2tog, K3, yo, S2K1P, yo, K3, SSK, yo) 8(9:10) times, SSM.

Lace round 33 (inc): (K1, M1P, P5, M1P, K1, yo, K2tog, yo, K3, S2K1P, K3, yo, SSK, yo) 8(9:10) times, SSM. (176(198:220) sts)

Lace round 34, 36, 38, &40: (K1, P7, K14) 8(9:10) times, SSM.

Lace round 35: (K1, P7, K1, yo, K2tog, K1, yo, K2, S2K1P, K2, yo, K1, SSK, yo) 8(9:10) times, SSM.

Lace round 37: (K1, P7, K1, yo, K2tog, K2, yo, K1, S2K1P, K1, yo, K2, SSK, yo) 8(9:10) times, SSM.

Lace round 39: (K1, P7, K1, yo, K2tog, K3, yo, S2K1P, yo, K3, SSK, yo) 8(9:10) times, SSM.

Lace round 41 (inc): (K1, M1P, P7, M1P, K1, yo, K2tog, yo, K3, S2K1P, K3, yo, SSK, yo) 8(9:10) times, SSM. (192(216:240) sts)

Lace round 42, 44, 46, & 48: (K1, P9, K14) 8(9:10) times, SSM.

Lace round 43: (K1, P9, K1, yo, K2tog, K1, yo, K2, S2K1P, K2, yo, K1, SSK, yo) 8(9:10) times, SSM.

Lace round 45: (K1, P9, K1, yo, K2tog, K2, yo, K1, S2K1P, K1, yo, K2, SSK, yo) 8(9:10) times, SSM.

Lace round 47: (K1, P9, K1, yo, K2tog, K3, yo, S2K1P, yo, K3, SSK, yo) 8(9:10) times, SSM.

Lace round 49 (inc): (K1, M1P, P9, M1P, K1, yo, K2tog, yo, K3, S2K1P, K3, yo, SSK, yo) 8(9:10) times, SSM. (208(234:260) sts)

Lace round 50, 52, 54, & 56: (K1, P11, K14) 8(9:10) times, SSM.

Lace round 51: (K1, P11, K1, yo, K2tog, K1, yo, K2, S2K1P, K2, yo, K1, SSK, yo) 8(9:10) times, SSM.

Lace round 53: (K1, P11, K1, yo, K2tog, K2, yo, K1, S2K1P, K1, yo, K2, SSK, yo) 8(9:10) times, SSM.

Lace round 55: (K1, P11, K1, yo, K2tog, K3, yo, S2K1P, yo, K3, SSK, yo) 8(9:10) times, SSM.

Lace round 57 (inc): (K1, M1P, P11, M1P, K1, yo, K2tog, yo, K3, S2K1P, K3, yo, SSK, yo) 8(9:10) times, SSM. (224(252:280) sts)

Lace round 58, 60, 62, & 64: (K1, P13, K14) 8(9:10) times, SSM.

Lace round 59: (K1, P13, K1, yo, K2tog, K1, yo, K2, S2K1P, K2, yo, K1, SSK, yo) 8(9:10) times, SSM.

Lace round 61: (K1, P13, K1, yo, K2tog, K2, yo, K1, S2K1P, K1, yo, K2, SSK, yo) 8(9:10) times, SSM.

Lace round 63: (K1, P13, K1, yo, K2tog, K3, yo, S2K1P, yo, K3, SSK, yo) 8(9:10) times, SSM.

Lace round 65 (inc): (K1, M1P, P13, M1P, K1, yo, K2tog, yo, K3, S2K1P, K3, yo, SSK, yo) 8(9:10) times, SSM. (240(270:300) sts)

Lace round 66, 68, 70, & 72: (K1, P15, K14) 8(9:10) times, SSM.

Lace round 67: (K1, P15, K1, yo, K2tog, K1, yo, K2, S2K1P, K2, yo, K1, SSK, yo) 8(9:10) times, SSM.

Lace round 69: (K1, P15, K1, yo, K2tog, K2, yo, K1, S2K1P, K1, yo, K2, SSK, yo) 8(9:10) times, SSM.

Lace round 71: (K1, P15, K1, yo, K2tog, K3, yo, S2K1P, yo, K3, SSK, yo) 8(9:10) times, SSM.

Lace round 73: (K1, P15, K1, yo, K2tog, yo, K3, S2K1P, K3, yo, SSK, yo) 8(9:10) times, SSM.
Work the last 8 rounds once more.

Now work edging as folls:
Edging row 1: Knit, SSM.
Edging row 2: Purl, SSM.
Edging row 3: (yo, K2tog) 120(135:150) times, SSM.
Edging row 4: Purl, SSM.
Edging row 5: Knit, SSM.

Turn work and cast off on WS working picot cast off as folls: Cast off 5 sts, *slip st on RH needle back onto LH needle, cast on 2 sts, then cast off 7 sts, rep from * to end.

MAKING UP
Sew in ends.
Press/block capelet as described on page 138. ✿

HATTIE
Elegant Mittens

Growing up, I spent many happy weekends and holiday afternoons watching old movies. Today I am conscious that the elegant women and the costumes from these movies inspire my design work. I love exploring detail with hand-knitting; I love the way that the stitches in this mitten pattern can be manipulated to create such a sophisticated shape, the design flowing effortlessly from the hem to the cast-off. This attention to detail for me is essential.

ONE SIZE
Width approx. 20 cm (8 in)
(measurement taken before thumb shaping)

YARN
Knitted in Double Knitting–weight yarn
Gauntlet mittens: Photographed using 2 x 50g/110m (1.75oz/120yd) hanks of Louisa Harding *Orielle* in 10 Jewel
Short mittens: Photographed using 1 x 50g/250m (1.75oz/273yd) ball Louisa Harding *Amitola* in 108 Hummingbird

NEEDLES
Pair of 3.25 mm (US 3) knitting needles
Pair of 4 mm (US 6) knitting needles

TENSION/GAUGE
22 sts x 30 rows to 10 cm (4 in) square measured over st st using 4 mm (US 6) knitting needles.

SPECIAL ABBREVIATIONS
C4B – slip 2 sts onto a cable needle, hold at back, K2, K2 from cable needle.
C4F – slip 2 sts onto a cable needle, hold at front, K2, K2 from cable needle.
SSK – slip 2 sts knitwise one at a time from the LH needle to the RH needle,
insert LH needle tip through both front loops and knit together.

NOTE
I have designed these mittens to be knitted flat then seamed.
The experienced knitter can easily convert the mittens to being knitted in the round by decreasing the stitch count by two and not including the selvedge edge stitches.

Hattie Elegant Mittens

Knitting with Amitola

The short mittens are knitted from 1 ball of Amitola yarn. To achieve a similar gradating effect on each mitten I knitted one mitten using yarn starting at the outside of the ball. To knit the second mitten I found the centre of the ball, discarded yarn until a similar shade was at the start as the first mitten and knitted the second mitten.

I advise using the cable cast on method with Amitola as the yarn is single spun and constant twisting of the yarn to cast on using the thumb method will result in the yarn losing strength and breaking.

Gauntlet mittens

Right hand

Using 4 mm (US 6) needles and using the cable cast on method cast on 71 sts.

Foundation row 1 (RS): Knit.
Foundation row 2: Knit.
Foundation row 3 (eyelets): K2, (yo, K2tog) 34 times, K1.
Foundation row 4: Knit.

*Work 32 rows in lace patt as folls:
Lace row 1 (RS): K1, (K3, K2tog, K3, yo, P7, yo, P3, SSK, K3) 3 times, K1.
Lace row 2, 4, 6 & 8: K1, (P8, K7, P8) 3 times, K1.
Lace row 3: K1, (K2, K2tog, K3, yo, K1, P7, K1, yo, P3, SSK, K2) 3 times, K1.
Lace row 5: K1, (K1, K2tog, K3, yo, K2, P7, K2, yo, P3, SSK, K1) 3 times, K1.
Lace row 7: K1, (K2tog, K3, yo, K3, P7, K3, yo, P3, SSK) 3 times, K1.

Lace row 9 (dec): K1, (K3, K2tog, K3, yo, P2tog, P3, P2tog, yo, P3, SSK, K3) 3 times, K1. (65 sts)
Lace row 10, 12, 14 & 16: K1, (P8, K5, P8) 3 times, K1.
Lace row 11: K1, (K2, K2tog, K3, yo, K1, P5, K1, yo, P3, SSK, K2) 3 times, K1.
Lace row 13: K1, (K1, K2tog, K3, yo, K2, P5, K2, yo, P3, SSK, K1) 3 times, K1.
Lace row 15: K1, (K1, K2tog, K3, yo, K2, P5, K2, yo, P3, SSK, K1) 3 times, K1.

Lace row 17 (dec): K1, (K3, K2tog, K3, yo, P2tog, P1, P2tog, yo, P3, SSK, K3) 3 times, K1. (59 sts)
Lace row 18, 20, 22 & 24: K1, (P8, K3, P8) 3 times, K1.
Lace row 19: K1, (K2, K2tog, K3, yo, K1, P3, K1, yo, P3, SSK, K2) 3 times, K1.
Lace row 21: K1, (K1, K2tog, K3, yo, K2, P3, K2, yo, P3, SSK, K1) 3 times, K1.
Lace row 23: K1, (K1, K2tog, K3, yo, K2, P3, K2, yo, P3, SSK, K1) 3 times, K1.

Lace row 25 (dec): K1, (K3, K2tog, K3, yo, P3tog, yo, P3, SSK, K3) 3 times, K1. (53 sts)
Lace row 26, 28 & 30: K1, (P8, K1, P8) 3 times, K1.
Lace row 27: K1, (K2, K2tog, K3, yo, K1, P1, K1, yo, P3, SSK, K2) 3 times, K1.
Lace row 29: K1, (K1, K2tog, K3, yo, K2, P1, K2, yo, P3, SSK, K1) 3 times, K1.
Lace row 31: K1, (K1, K2tog, K3, yo, K2, P1, K2, yo, P3, SSK, K1) 3 times, K1.
Lace row 32 (dec): K1, (P4, K2tog, P2tog, K1, P2tog, K2tog, P4) 3 times, K1. (41 sts)

Now work 26 rounds in cable and rib patt setting sts as folls:
Cable row 1: K1, (K4, P1, [K1, P1] twice, K4) 3 times, K1.
Cable row 2: K1, (P4, K1, [P1, K1] twice, P4) 3 times, K1.
Cable row 3: K1, (K4, P1, [K1, P1] twice, K4) 3 times, K1.
Cable row 4: K1, (P4, K1, [P1, K1] twice, P4) 3 times, K1.

Cable row 5: K1, (C4F, P1, [K1, P1] twice, C4B) 3 times, K1.
Cable row 6: K1, (P4, K1, [P1, K1] twice, P4) 3 times, K1.
Cable row 7: K1, (K4, P1, [K1, P1] twice, K4) 3 times, K1.
Cable row 8: K1, (P4, K1, [P1, K1] twice, P4) 3 times, K1.
The last 4 rows form the cable and rib patt rep.
Work these 4 rows 4 times more.
Work cable row 5 once more.

Next row (WS)(dec): K1, P2tog, P2, (K1, [P1, K1] twice, P3, P2tog, P3) twice, K1, (P1, K1) twice, P4, K1.
(38 sts)

Beg with a K row work 8 rows in st st with selvedge edge st as folls:
Row 1: Knit.
Row 2: K1, P36, K1.
Work a further 6 rows in patt as set.*

Shape thumb

Row 1 (RS)(inc): K20, M1, K3, M1, K15. (40 sts)
Work 3 rows in patt.
Row 5 (RS)(inc): K20, M1, K5, M1, K15. (42 sts)
Work 3 rows in patt.
Cont in st st and inc as above on next row and every foll 4th row to 48 sts.
Work 1 row in patt, ending with RS facing for next row.

Cast off for thumb

Next row (RS)(dec): K20, cast off 2 sts, (slip last st on RH needle back onto LH needle, cast on 2 sts, cast off 4 sts) 5 times, (21 sts on RH needle), K15. (36 sts)
Next row (WS)(dec): K1, P13, P2tog, P19, K1. (35 sts)

Hattie Elegant Mittens

**Beg with a K row work 14 rows in st st with selvedge edge st as before ending with RS facing for next row. Change to 3.25 mm (US 3) needles and work 5 rows in eyelet edging as folls:
Edging row 1 (RS): Knit.
Edging row 2: Knit.
Edging row 3 (eyelets): K2, (yo, K2tog) 16 times, K1.
Edging row 4: Knit.
Edging row 5: Knit.
Cast off on WS using the picot cast off method as folls:
Cast off 2 sts, (slip st on RH needle back onto LH needle, cast on 2 sts, cast off 5 sts) 11 times.**

Left hand

Using 4 mm (US 6) needles and using the cable cast on method cast on 71 sts.
Foundation row 1 (RS): Knit.
Foundation row 2: Knit.
Foundation row 3 (eyelets): K2, (yo, K2tog) 34 times, K1.
Foundation row 4: Knit.
Work as for right hand from * to *.

Shape thumb

Row 1 (RS): K15, M1, K3, M1, K20. (40 sts)
Work 3 rows in patt.
Row 5 (RS): K15, M1, K5, M1, K20. (42 sts)
Work 3 rows in patt.
Cont in st st and inc as above on next row and every foll 4th row to 48 sts.
Work 1 row in patt, ending with RS facing for next row.

Cast off for thumb

Next row (RS)(dec): K15, cast off 2 sts, (slip last st on RH needle back onto LH needle, cast on 2 sts, cast off 4 sts) 5 times, (16 sts on RH needle), K20. (36 sts)
Next row (WS)(dec): K1, P19, P2tog, P13, K1. (35 sts)
Work as for right hand mitten from ** to **.

Making up

Sew in all ends.
Press/block as described on page 138.
Sew side seams together using mattress stitch or back stitch if preferred taking knit stitch selvedge into seam.

Short mittens

Right hand

Using 4 mm (US 6) needles and using the cable cast on method cast on 59 sts.
Foundation row 1 (RS): Knit.
Foundation row 2: Knit.
Foundation row 3 (eyelets): K2, (yo, K2tog) 28 times, K1.
Foundation row 4: Knit.
Starting with lace row 19 work 16 rows in lace patt as for right hand gauntlet and continuing to end.

Left hand

Using 4 mm (US 6) needles and using the cable cast on method cast on 59 sts.
Foundation row 1 (RS): Knit.
Foundation row 2: Knit.
Foundation row 3 (eyelets): K2, (yo, K2tog) 28 times, K1.
Foundation row 4: Knit.
Starting with lace row 19 work 16 rows in lace patt as for left hand gauntlet and continuing to end.

BONNIE
BUTTERFLY VEST

As a knitwear designer I love the challenge of approaching ideas from different angles. This vest uses an undulating cast-on edge created by the lace pattern as the sleeve edges. Two identical pieces are worked and turned ninety degrees, and seams are sewn at the lower edge transforming the knitted pieces into a garment. The addition of a ribbon threaded through the eyelets emphasises the feminine figure.

THREE SIZES
Actual size: 78cm (30¾ in), 88 cm (34½ in), 98 cm (38½ in)
Finished length: 47 cm (17½ in)

YARN
Knitted in Double Knitting–weight yarn
Photographed using 5, 6, 7 x 50g/110m (1.75oz/120yd) hanks of Louisa Harding *Orielle* in 18 Conserve

NEEDLES
Pair of 4 mm (US 6) knitting needles 10 stitch markers

EXTRAS
2 metres (79 in) of wide gauze ribbon

TENSION/GAUGE
21 sts x 32 rows to 10 cm (4 in) square measured over lace patt using 4 mm (US 6) knitting needles.

SPECIAL ABBREVIATIONS
SSK – slip 2 sts knitwise one at a time from the LH needle to the RH needle,
insert LH needle tip through both front loops and knit together.
SSM – Slip stitch marker.

NOTE
This garment is knitted from side to side in two identical pieces. It is the number of stitches cast on that determines the garment's length and the number of row pattern repeats worked that determines the garment's width.

Bonnie Butterfly Vest

Left front/back
Using 4 mm (US 6) needles cast on 198 sts.

Foundation row 1 (RS): K23, place stitch marker, (K17, place stitch marker) 9 times, K22.

Foundation row 2: K22, slip stitch marker - SSM, (K17, SSM) 9 times, K23.

Foundation row 3: K23, SSM, (K1, [yo, K2tog] 8 times, SSM) 9 times, K22.

Foundation row 4: K22, SSM, (K17, SSM) 9 times, K23.

Work 8 rows in lace and garter st eyelet edging setting sts as folls:

Patt row 1 (RS): K22, P1, SSM, (yo, K3, SSK, K6, K2tog, K3, yo, P1, SSM) 9 times, K22.

Patt row 2, 4 & 6: K22, SSM, (P17, SSM) 9 times, P1, K22.

Patt row 3: K3, [yo, K2tog] 9 times, K1, P1, SSM, (K1, yo, K3, SSK, K4, K2tog, K3, yo, K1, P1, SSM) 9 times, K2, [yo, K2tog] 9 times, K2.

Patt row 5: K22, P1, SSM, (K2, yo, K3, SSK, K2, K2tog, K3, yo, K2, P1, SSM) 9 times, K22.

Patt row 7: K22, P1, SSM, (K3, yo, K3, SSK, K2tog, K3, yo, K3, P1, SSM) 9 times, K22.

Patt row 8: K22, SSM, (P17, SSM) 9 times, P1, K22.

These 8 rows form the lace and garter st eyelet edging patt and are worked throughout.

Work these 8 rows 6(7:8) times more, ending with patt row 8.

Work dec row as folls:
Next row (RS)(dec): K21, P2tog, SSM, (K3, SSK, K6, K2tog, K3, P1, SSM) 9 times, K22. (179 sts)

Next row (WS): Knit across row removing stitch markers.
Next row: Knit.
Next row: Knit.
Next row: K3, [yo, K2tog] to last 2 sts, K2.
Next row: Knit.
Next row: Knit.
Cast off knitwise on WS, taking care not to pull sts too tightly.

Right front/back
Work as for left front/back.

Making up
Sew in ends.
Press/block pieces as described on page 138.

Turn all pieces ninety degrees so that the cast on edges (fluted edge) become the sleeve edge, the cast off edges (straight edge) become the centre back and front edges. The garter stitch edge either side of the lace pattern becomes the bottom of the garment. Using the photographs as a guide, construct the garment as folls:

Back seam
Lay right back and left back together with straight sides together. Starting at cast off edges measure 28 cm (11 in) up from cast off edge, join seam for back using mattress stitch or back stitch if preferred.

Right side seam
Stitch together the garter stitch edging for front and back using mattress stitch or back stitch if preferred.

Left side seam
Stitch together the garter stitch edging for front and back using mattress stitch or back stitch if preferred.

Starting at right centre front, thread ribbon through the eyelets above garter st edging to left centre front, tie with a bow. ◉

VELMA
Wispy Shrug

This little shrug is the perfect pair of sleeves. Knitted using a wispy, light double knitting–weight yarn in a lovely chevron and lace pattern which showcases the variegation beautifully, this design is just perfect to slip over a simple dress when the cool spring or autumn breezes start to swirl.

THREE SIZES
Cuff to cuff: 127 cm (50 in), 132 cm (52 in), 137 cm (54 in)
Centre back neck to hem: 49.5 cm (19½ in)

YARN
③
Knitted in Double Knitting–weight yarn
Photographed using 2, 3, 3 x 50g/250m (1.75oz/273yd) balls of Louisa Harding *Amitola* in 113 Pot Pourri

NEEDLES
Pair of 4.5 mm (US 7) knitting needles

TENSION/GAUGE
25 sts x 26 rows to 10 cm (4 in) square measured over chevron pattern using 4.5 mm (US 7) knitting needles.
20 sts x 30 rows to 10 cm (4 in) square measured lace patt using 4.5 mm (US 7) knitting needles.

SPECIAL ABBREVIATIONS
S2KP – slip 2 sts together from LH needle to RH needle (as if knitting them together), K1, pass the 2 slipped stitches over the stitch knitted.
SSK – slip 2 sts knitwise one at a time from the LH needle to the RH needle, insert LH needle tip through both front loops and knit together.

Velma Wispy Shrug

Knitting with Amitola

When choosing yarn for this project select balls which start with the same colour. To get a similar gradating effect on both sleeves start each sleeve of the shrug with a separate ball.

To avoid any strong colour striping, once you have completed your first ball of yarn, ensure the next ball you use starts with a similar colour to the one just finished.

Left sleeve and left back

Using 4.5 mm (US 7) needles work picot cast on as folls:
*Cast on 5 sts using the cable cast on method,
cast off 2 sts, slip st on RH needle back onto LH needle*
(3 sts now on LH needle), rep from * to * 24 times more.
(75 sts)

Foundation row 1 (RS): Knit.
Foundation row 2: Knit.
Foundation row 3 (dec): K1, K2tog, (K9, S2KP) 5 times, K9, SSK, K1. (63 sts)
Foundation row 4: Knit.

Work 10 rows in chevron and garter st edging setting sts as folls:

Edging row 1 (RS): K1, K2tog, (K3, yo, K1, yo, K3, S2KP) 5 times, K3, yo, K1, yo, K3, SSK, K1.
Edging row 2: Knit.
These 2 rows form the edging patt.
Rep these 2 rows 4 times more.

Now work in chevron and st st patt setting sts as folls:

Patt row 1 (RS): K1, K2tog, (K3, yo, K1, yo, K3, S2KP) 5 times, K3, yo, K1, yo, K3, SSK, K1.
Patt row 2: K1, P to last st, K1.
These 2 rows form the chevron and st st patt with garter st edgings.

Rep these 2 rows until work measures 43 cm (17 in) from cast on edge measured at the longest point (side edge), ending with RS facing for next row, place a marker at each end to mark end of sleeves.

Now work lace with garter st and picot edging patt increasing at side edges as folls:

Inc row 1 (RS)(inc): K6, yo, K1, (K3, yo, S2KP, yo, K4) 5 times, yo, K6. (65 sts)
Inc row 2: K8, (P9, K16 5 times, K7.

Inc row 3 (inc)(picot): Cast on 2 sts, cast off 2 sts (1 st on RH needle) K5, yo, K2, (K1, K2tog, yo, K3, yo, SSK, K2) 5 times, K1, yo, K6. (67 sts)
Inc row 4 (picot): Cast on 2 sts, cast off 2 sts (1 st on RH needle) K8, (P9, K1) 5 times, K8.

Inc row 5 (inc): K6, yo, K3, (K2tog, yo, K5, yo, SSK, K1) 5 times, K2, yo, K6. (69 sts)
Inc row 6: K10, (P9, K1) 5 times, K9.

Inc row 7 (inc)(picot): Cast on 2 sts, cast off 2 sts (1 st on RH needle) K5, yo, K4, (K2, yo, SSK, K1, K2tog, yo, K3) 5 times, K3, yo, K6. (71 sts)
Inc row 8 (picot): Cast on 2 sts, cast off 2 sts (1 st on RH needle) K10, (P9, K1) 5 times, K10.

Inc row 9 (inc): K6, yo, K5, (K3, yo, S2KP, yo, K4) 5 times, K4, yo, K6. (73 sts)
Inc row 10: K12, (P9, K1) 5 times, K11.

Inc row 11 (inc)(picot): Cast on 2 sts, cast off 2 sts (1 st on RH needle) K5, yo, K6, (K1, K2tog, yo, K3, yo, SSK, K2) 5 times, K5, yo, K6. (75 sts)
Inc row 12 (picot): Cast on 2 sts, cast off 2 sts (1 st on RH needle) K12, (P9, K1) 5 times, K12.

Inc row 13 (inc): K6, yo, K7, (K2tog, yo, K5, yo, SSK, K1) 5 times, K6, yo, K6. (77 sts)
Inc row 14: K14, (P9, K1) 5 times, K13.

Inc row 15 (inc)(picot): Cast on 2 sts, cast off 2 sts (1 st on RH needle) K5, yo, K8, (K2, yo, SSK, K1, K2tog, yo, K3) 5 times, K7, yo, K6. (79 sts)
Inc row 16 (picot): Cast on 2 sts, cast off 2 sts (1 st on RH needle) K14, (P9, K1) 5 times, K14.

Now work 8 rows in lace with garter st and picot edging patt as folls:

Patt row 1: K6, yo, K2tog, K7, (K3, yo, S2KP, yo, K4) 5 times, K6, SSK, yo, K6.
Patt row 2: K15, (P9, K1) 5 times, K14.

Patt row 3 (picot): Cast on 2 sts, cast off 2 sts (1 st on RH needle) K5, yo, K2tog, K7, (K1, K2tog, yo, K3, yo, SSK, K2) 5 times, K6, SSK, yo, K6.
Patt row 4 (picot): Cast on 2 sts, cast off 2 sts (1 st on RH needle) K14, (P9, K1) 5 times, K14.

Patt row 5: K6, yo, K2tog, K7, (K2tog, yo, K5, yo, SSK, K1) 5 times, K6, SSK, yo, K6.
Patt row 6: K15, (P9, K1) 5 times, K14.

Patt row 7 (picot): Cast on 2 sts, cast off 2 sts (1 st on RH needle) K5, yo, K2tog, K7, (K2, yo, SSK, K1, K2tog, yo, K3) 5 times, K6, SSK, yo, K6.
Patt row 8 (picot): Cast on 2 sts, cast off 2 sts (1 st on RH needle) K14, (P9, K1) 5 times, K14.
Rep these 8 rows until work measures approx. 20.5(23:25.5) cm (8(9:10) in) from end of sleeve marker ending with patt row 1 and WS facing for next row. **
Leave these sts on a spare needle.

Right sleeve and right back
Work as for left sleeve and left back to **.

Making up
Sew in all ends.
Press/block pieces as described on page 138.

With RS together join both pieces of work by either grafting the stitches together or knitting together the stitches on the WS from both holders using the three needle cast off.

Left sleeve
Sew together row ends of left sleeve from cast on edge to sleeve end marker.

Right sleeve
Sew together row ends of right sleeve from cast on edge to sleeve end marker.

NORA
DAZZLE SCARVES

Like many knitters, I often feel conflicted about which yarn to choose for a certain design, idea or project. For this simple eight-row cable and lace pattern I decided to show two variations, one knitted in a whispery gossamer variegated yarn, the other in a gloriously self-beaded yarn. The result is two beautifully different scarves, one light and feathery, the other drapey and dazzling.

SIZE
Variegated scarf: Approx. 23 cm (9 in) wide x 172 cm (67½ in) long
Beaded scarf: Approx. 18 cm (7 in) wide x 81.5 cm (32 in) long

YARN
(3)
Variegated scarf: Knitted in Double Knitting–weight yarn
Photographed using 2 x 50g/250m (1.75oz/273yd) balls of Louisa Harding *Amitola* in 114 Dawn
(4)
Beaded scarf: Knitted in Aran-weight yarn
Photographed using 3 x 50g/67.5m (1.75oz/74yd) hanks of Louisa Harding *Grace Hand Beaded* in 36 Palma

NEEDLES
Variegated scarf: Pair of 4 mm (US 6) knitting needles Pair of 4.5 mm (US 7) knitting needles Cable needle
Beaded scarf: Pair of 4.5 mm (US 7) knitting needles Pair of 5 mm (US 8) knitting needles Cable needle

TENSION/GAUGE
Variegated scarf: 20 sts x 28 rows to 10 cm (4 in) square measured over cable and lace patt
using 4.5 mm (US 7) knitting needles.
Beaded scarf: 18 sts x 24 rows to 10 cm (4 in) square measured over cable and lace patt
using 5 mm (US 8) knitting needles.

SPECIAL ABBREVIATIONS
S2KP – slip 2 sts onto RH needle as if going to knit them together, K1,
pass the 2 slipped stitches over the knitted stitch.
SSK – slip 2 sts knitwise one at a time from the LH needle to the RH needle,
insert LH needle tip through both front loops and knit together.
C6B – slip 3 sts onto a cable needle, hold at back, K3, K3 from cable needle.

Nora Dazzle Scarves

Knitting with Amitola

To avoid any strong colour striping, once you have completed your first ball of yarn, ensure the next ball you use starts with a similar colour to the one just finished.

Variegated scarf

Using 4 mm (US 6) needles work picot cast on as folls:
Cast on 5 sts using the cable cast on method, cast off 2 sts, slip st on RH needle back onto LH needle (3 sts now on LH needle), rep from * to * 17 times more. (54 sts)

Foundation row 1 (RS): Knit.
Foundation row 2: Knit.
Foundation row 3 (eyelets): K2, (yo, K2tog) 25 times, K2.
Foundation row 4: Knit.

Change to 4.5 mm (US 7) needles and work 8 rows in cable and lace patt setting sts as folls:

Patt row 1 (RS)(inc): K5, yo, K2tog, K2, (K7, K2tog, yo, K5, yo, SSK, K1) twice, K8, yo, K3. (55 sts)
Patt row 2: K6, (P6, K1, P9, K1) twice, P6, K2, P2, K5.
Patt row 3 (inc): K5, yo, K2tog, K2, (K9, yo, SSK, K1, K2tog, yo, K3) twice, K8, yo, K4. (56 sts)
Patt row 4: K7, (P6, K1, P9, K1) twice, P6, K2, P2, K5.
Patt row 5 (inc)(cable): K5, yo, K2tog, K2, (C6B, K4, yo, S2KP, yo, K4) twice, C6B, K2, yo, K5. (57 sts)
Patt row 6: K8, (P6, K1, P9, K1) twice, P6, K2, P2, K5.
Patt row 7 (inc): K5, yo, K2tog, K2, (K8, K2tog, yo, K3, yo, SSK, K2) twice, K8, yo, K6. (58 sts)
Patt row 8 (dec): cast off 4 sts, (1 st on LH needle), K4, (P6, K1, P9, K1) twice, P6, K2, P2, K5. (54 sts)
These 8 rows form the cable and lace patt.
Work these 8 rows 60 times more, ending with patt row 8.

Change to 4 mm (US 6) needles and work edging as folls:
Edging row 1 (RS): Knit.
Edging row 2: Knit.
Edging row 3 (eyelets): K2, (yo, K2tog) 25 times, K2.
Edging row 4: Knit.
Edging row 5: Knit.
Cast off using the picot cast off method as folls:
Cast off 3 sts, *slip st on RH needle back onto LH needle, cast on 2 sts, then cast off 5 sts, rep from * 17 times more, cast off to end.

Making up

Sew in all ends.
Press/block scarf as described on page 138.

Beaded scarf

Using 4.5 mm (US 7) needles work picot cast on as folls:
Cast on 5 sts using the cable cast on method, cast off 2 sts, slip st on RH needle back onto LH needle (3 sts now on LH needle), rep from * to * 11 times more, cast on 1 st. (37 sts)

Foundation row 1 (RS): Knit.
Foundation row 2: Knit.
Foundation row 3 (eyelets): K1, (yo, K2tog) 17 times, K2.
Foundation row 4: Knit.

Change to 5 mm (US 6) needles and work 8 rows in cable and lace patt setting sts as folls:

Patt row 1 (RS)(inc): K5, yo, K2tog, K9, K2tog, yo, K5, yo, SSK, K9, yo, K3. (38 sts)
Patt row 2: K6, P6, K1, P9, K1, P6, K2, P2, K5.
Patt row 3 (inc): K5, yo, K2tog, K11, yo, SSK, K1, K2tog, yo, K11, yo, K4. (39 sts)
Patt row 4: K7, P6, K1, P9, K1, P6, K2, P2, K5.
Patt row 5 (inc)(cable): K5, yo, K2tog, K2, C6B, K4, yo, S2KP, yo, K4, C6B, K2, yo, K5. (40 sts)
Patt row 6: K8, P6, K1, P9, K1, P6, K2, P2, K5.
Patt row 7 (inc): K5, yo, K2tog, K10, K2tog, yo, K3, yo, SSK, K10, yo, K6. (41 sts)
Patt row 8 (dec): cast off 4 sts, (1 st on LH needle), K4, P6, K1, P9, K1, P6, K2, P2, K5. (37 sts)
These 8 rows form the cable and lace patt.
Work these 8 rows 23 times more, ending with patt row 8.

Change to 4.5 mm (US 7) needles and work edging as folls:
Edging row 1 (RS): Knit.
Edging row 2: Knit.
Edging row 3 (eyelets): K1, (yo, K2tog) 17 times, K2.
Edging row 4: Knit.
Edging row 5: Knit.
Cast off using the picot cast off method as folls:
Cast off 3 sts, *slip st on RH needle back onto LH needle, cast on 2 sts, then cast off 5 sts, rep from * 10 times more, cast off to end.

Making up

Sew in all ends.
Press/block scarf as described on page 138.

General Information

The projects in this book have been designed to work with my very own range of yarns. I have created patterns that I hope will appeal to a wide range of knitters, from those picking up knitting needles for the first time to begin their first project to more experienced knitters looking for that special pattern. To create interest for the knitter I have used combinations of yarns together in the same design as well as different knitted edgings, cables, picot cast-ons and knitted additions. In this section you will find information on how to read the patterns and to finish off your project beautifully as well as information regarding different yarn types and how to substitute the suggested yarns.

The knitting patterns
Each pattern has written instructions laid out as follows:

Sizes
At the beginning of each pattern you will find the measurements for the finished project. Many of the projects are accessories, hats, mittens and scarves, so the measurements given are approximate as the items are designed to stretch when worn. If your chosen pattern is multi-sized all the widths and lengths are listed.

Yarn
This indicates the weight of yarn (e.g., worsted) and amount needed to complete the design. All of the projects that use more than one shade of yarn will include a quantity for each shade used. The quantities of yarn are based on average requirements and are therefore approximate.

Needles
Listed are the suggested knitting needles to make the project. The smaller needles are usually used for edgings or ribs, the larger needles for the main fabric of the work. You might need to use different needles to achieve the gauge or tension stated in the pattern.

Extras
This indicates the additional items you may require to finish your project.

Tension/Gauge
This is the single most important factor when you begin knitting. The fabric tension is written as, for example, '22 sts x 30 rows to 10 cm (4 in) measured over stocking stitch (stockinette stitch) using 4 mm (US 6) needles.'
Each pattern is worked out mathematically; If the correct tension is not achieved, the project will not fit as intended. Before embarking on knitting your project, we recommend that you check your tension as follows: Using the needle size suggested, cast on 5–10 more stitches than stated in the tension specification paragraph and work 5–10 more rows than stated.
When you have knitted your tension square, lay it on a flat surface, place a rule or tape measure across it horizontally, and count the number of stitches that fall within a 10 cm (4 in) space. Place the measure vertically up the piece and count the number of rows. These figures should equal those stated in the pattern tension note. If you have too many stitches to 10 cm (4 in), try again using a larger needle; if you have too few stitches to 10 cm (4 in), use a smaller needle.

Note: Check your gauge regularly as you knit; once you become relaxed and confident with your knitting, your gauge can change.

Instructions
Instructions are given for the first size, with larger sizes in parentheses. Where only one figure or instruction is given, instructions apply to all sizes.

Abbreviations

Check your chosen project as you may find a special abbreviation note. Some of the most common words used have been abbreviated as listed:

K	knit
P	purl
st(s)	stitch(es)
inc	increase(e)(ing), knit into the front and back of next st to make two stitches
dec	decreas(e)(ing), work two sts together to make one stitch
st st	stockinette stitch (right side row knit, wrong side row purl)
garter st	garter stitch (knit every row)
beg	begin(ning)
foll	follow(s)(ing)
rem	remain(ing)
rev	reverse(ing)
rep	repeat
alt	alternate
cont	continu(e)(ing)
patt	pattern
tog	together
cm	centimeter(s)
in(s)	inch(es)
RS	right side
WS	wrong side
K2tog	knit two sts together to make one stitch
tbl	through back of loop
yo	yarn over, bring yarn over needle before working next st to create an extra loop
Sl1	slip one stitch
psso	pass slipped stitch over
M1	make one stitch by picking up horizontal loop before next stitch and knitting into back of it
M1P	make one stitch by picking up horizontal loop before next stitch and purling into back of it
Kwise	Knitwise
C4(6, 8, 10)F	Slip next 2(3, 4, 5) sts onto a cable needle, hold at front of work, knit 2(3, 4, 5) sts, knit 2(3, 4, 5) sts from cable needle.
C4(6, 8, 10)B	Slip next 2(3, 4, 5) sts onto a cable needle, hold at back of work, knit 2(3, 4, 5) sts, knit 2(3, 4, 5) sts from cable needle.

USA Glossary

UK	USA
Cast off	Bind off
Tension	Gauge
Stocking stitch	Stockinette stitch
Moss stitch	Seed stitch

Finishing Techniques

After you spend many hours knitting, it is essential that you complete your project correctly. With these simple written instructions, we will show you how easy it is to achieve a beautifully finished accessory.

Pressing - For natural fibers.
With the wrong side of the fabric facing, pin out each knitted piece onto an ironing board using the measurements given as a guide. As each yarn is different, refer to the ball band and press the pieces according to the instructions given. Pressing the knitted fabric will help the pieces maintain their shape and give a smooth finish.

Blocking - For synthetic fibers.
With the wrong side of the fabric facing, pin out each knitted piece onto a blocking or ironing board using the measurements given as a guide. Cover each piece with a cloth (e.g., tea towel), and using a water spray, spray the cloth until damp. Leave the cloth on top of the knitted piece and allow it to dry completely. As each yarn is different, refer to the ball band and press the pieces according to the instructions given. Blocking the knitted fabric will help the pieces maintain their shape and give a smooth finish.

Sewing in ends - Once you have pressed your finished pieces, sew in all loose ends. Thread a darning needle with yarn, weave needle along approximately 5 sts on wrong side of fabric, and pull thread through. Weave needle in opposite direction approximately 5 sts, pull thread through, and cut end of yarn.

Mattress stitch - This method of sewing-up is worked on the right side of the fabric and is ideal for matching stripes. Mattress stitch should be worked one stitch in from the edge of the work to give the best finish. With RS of work facing, lay the two pieces to be joined edge to edge. Insert needle from WS between edge st and second st. Take yarn to opposite piece, insert needle from front, pass the needle under two rows, bring it back through to the front and insert it again into the opposite piece at the point of its last exit.

Back stitch - Pin the pieces with right sides together. Insert needle into fabric at end, one stitch or row from edge, and take the needle around the two edges to secure them. Insert needle into fabric just behind where last stitch came out and make a short stitch. Re-insert needle where previous stitch started, and bring up needle to make a longer stitch. Re-insert needle where last stitch ended. Repeat to end, taking care to match any pattern features.

Yarn Information

You can purchase yarns two ways: from the yarn shop, where you will find really helpful, knowledgeable staff and an amazing array of products: knitting yarns, needles, buttons, and beads, or from the Internet, where there are many really good yarn websites. You can find them easily when you put in a search for 'knitting yarns'. These sites often show the whole spectrum of colors in yarn ranges, have lots of information available, and are a fantastic resource. However, before you begin knitting, visit a yarn store so you can get an idea of what is available, as nothing compares with the tactile quality of touching and feeling a ball of yarn.

When you visit the yarn shop you will find a wide range of colors and textures. The choice is unbelievable, and you will feel like a kid in a candy shop. Choosing which yarn to use can be quite daunting; in the knitting patterns here I have specified the yarn used because it is often the texture and colors that inspire the design. In this book I have used a variety of different yarn types, some for practical reasons, some because of the color, texture, shine and quality. Below I have listed some of the yarns I have chosen along with their unique qualities and notes on availability.

Animal Fiber Yarns

WOOL - Wool is the traditional yarn that we knit with and comes from the fleece of sheep. Wool is very warm to wear, as it holds in the heat, and is great for accessories. Traditionally wool can be itchy and scratchy, and when you wear it close to the skin, as a hat, scarf or gloves, it can be quite uncomfortable. Many yarn spinners now make very soft wool blends using different types of fleece. I suggest you look for yarns made of merino wool blends, as these are the softest. Wool yarns can look different, depending on how they are spun. Woolen spun, which produces tweed yarns, is dyed before spinning, the color and texture added as the yarn is spun. Worsted spun is spun first and then dyed afterwards, producing a soft, continuous yarn that usually comes in many beautiful colors. This spinning process also works with synthetic yarn and yarn that is specially treated to make it machine washable. Look on the label for washing instructions. If you use a traditional wool yarn that is slightly coarse in texture, I suggest that after you have knitted it, you hand wash it with some fabric softener. This will make the fabric feel wonderfully soft.

CASHMERE - Cashmere is a luxury fiber, and pure cashmere yarns can be expensive. Because of this reality, many spinners combine it with wool to make it more affordable. These yarns feel wonderful to knit with, touch and wear.

SILK - Silk is a wonderful fiber and absorbs color when it is dyed to produce beautiful, vivid shades, however it is expensive to produce and thus is often mixed with other yarn fibers.

MOHAIR - Mohair comes from the Angora goat, and when spun, produces a light, fluffy and very warm yarn. Because it is hairy you can knit this yarn to the same gauge as a thicker yarn using bigger needles, and the hairy fibers give the fabric stability.

ANGORA - Angora comes from the Angora rabbit. The luxurious silky hairs are very short and difficult to spin without combining it with wool or synthetic fibers. As it is expensive to produce it is ideal for small projects. Do take care, as the short hairs in this yarn tend to shed and can cause an allergic reaction.

Vegetable Fiber Yarns

COTTON - Cotton yarns are now very popular and made from the cotton plant. The yarn is soft and non-itchy, which is good for sensitive skin, but it does not have much elasticity. I love the way cotton yarns when knitted enhance the texture of cables and stitch structures. When knitted it can be quite heavy, so it's ideal for small projects like purses. It is extremely important that, when knitting cotton, the correct gauge is obtained, otherwise the project will not wear well.

LINEN - Linen yarn is obtained from the flax plant. It is strong and extremely durable, but if knitted as a solid fiber it can be tough and resemble rope. This yarn is most often blended with other fibers to make it softer and less difficult to work with.

SYNTHETIC YARNS - Nylon, acrylic and viscose yarns are widely available in the marketplace. Made from man-made fibers, they come in many varieties, and you can find exciting, experimental yarns in wonderful colors. I especially love the metallic yarns that add sparkle and glamour to many fashions. These yarns are great, but there's a caveat: They will not have the long-lasting properties of natural yarns.

INTERCHANGEABLE YARN TABLE

I have designed and photographed the projects in this book using specific yarns as detailed in each pattern. As time goes by some yarns and shades may become discontinued and availability limited. If you are unable to locate the exact yarn detailed you will need to substitute the yarn. Below is a table of yarns from my yarn range that are interchangeable. The yarns are listed by the generic weight as given at the beginning of each pattern alongside of the yarns from my ranges which are interchangeable.

GENERIC WEIGHT

(3)

Double knitting–weight yarn   4 mm (US 6) needles   Average tension 22 sts x 30 rows
Louisa Harding Yarn - Grace*, Grace Hand Beaded*, Grace Harmonies*, Amitola, Orielle,
Mulberry, Mulberry Hand Beaded

(4)

Worsted-weight yarn   4.5 mm (US 7) needles   Average tension 20 sts x 26/28 rows
Louisa Harding Yarn - Grace*, Grace Hand Beaded*, Grace Harmonies*, Jesse

(4)

Aran-weight yarn   5 mm (US 8) needles   Average tension 18 sts x 24 rows
Louisa Harding Yarn - Akiko, Mila, Colline

(6)

Super Bulky–weight yarn 8 mm (US 11) needles Average tension 11/12 sts x 14/16 rows
Louisa Harding Yarn - Luzia, Sari Ribbon

* The Grace family of yarns can be knitted to either a generic Double Knitting–weight tension or a Worsted-weight tension. This is because the yarn is single spun and will fill out when knitted.

SUBSTITUTING YARNS

If you substitute a yarn not from the Louisa Harding range of yarns YOU MUST MATCH THE TENSION/GAUGE stated in the pattern. All the patterns in this book are worked out mathematically to the specified generic yarn weight. If the correct tension is not achieved your project will turn out too big or too small. The tension will be stated on the yarn label, and I strongly recommend that you knit a swatch of your chosen yarn before embarking on the design. Saying this, it can be fun to substitute yarns and starts you thinking creatively about knitting.

CONTACT

If you have any comments or enquiries please write to me at
E-mail: enquiries@louisaharding.co.uk   URL: www.louisaharding.co.uk

Yarn Distributors

The following companies distribute Louisa Harding Yarns.
Their websites have helpful information regarding yarns, shade cards and yarn store locators.

AUSTRALIA & NEW ZEALAND: Prestige Yarns Pty Ltd.
Tel: + 61 02 4285 6669   E-mail: infor@prestigeyarns.com   URL: www.prestigeyarns.com

CANADA: Diamond Yarns Ltd.
Tel: 001 416 736 6111 Fax: 001 416 736 6112   URL: www.diamondyarns.com

DEUTSCHLAND, AUSTRIA, SWITZERLAND, BELGIUM, NETHERLANDS & LUXEMBURG: Designer Yarns Ltd.
Tel: + 49 (0) 2203 1021910 Fax: + 49 (0) 2203 1023551 E-mail: info@designeryarns.de URL: www.designeryarns.de

FRANCE: Plassard Diffusion
Tel: +33 (0) 385 28 28 29 E-mail: info@laines-plassard.com URL: www.laines-plassard.com

ICELAND: Storkurrin
Tel no: 354 551 8258 Fax no: 354 562 8252   E-mail: storkurinn@storkurinn.is

KUWAIT: Agricultural Aquarium Co
Tel no: 0965 66757070 E-mail: computerscience2003@gmail.com

POLAND: AmiQs
Tel no: 00 486 006 41001 E-mail: marcin@ittec.pl

PORTUGAL: Knitting Labs
Tel: + 35 191 728 1659 E-mail: luisa.arruda@knittinglabs.com URL: www.knittinglabs.com

RUSSIA: Golden Fleece.
Tel: + 7(495) 967 1547 E-mail: info@rukodelie.ru URL: www.rukodelie.ru

SINGAPORE: Quilts n Calicoes
Tel no: 65 688 74708   E-mail: quiltchick@quiltsncalicoes.com

SOUTH KOREA: AnnKnitting
Tel: +82 70 4367 2779 Fax: +82 2 6937 0577 E-mail: tedd@annknitting.com URL: www.annknitting.com

SPAIN: Almacenes Castelltort
Tel: 93 268 3611 (900 805 222 Fuera de Barcelona) Fax: 93 268 11 17
E-mail: comercial@castelltort.com   URL: www.castelltort.com

SWEDEN & NORWAY: Modeknappen.
Tel: + 46 524 23310   Fax + 46 524 23110   E-mail: info@modeknappen.se URL: www.modeknappen.se

UK & IRELAND: Designer Yarns Ltd.
Tel: +44 (0)1535 664222 Fax: +44 (0)1535 664333
E-mail: alex@designeryarns.uk.com   URL: www.designeryarns.uk.com

USA: Knitting Fever Inc.
Tel: 001 516 546 3600 Fax: 001 516 546 6871   E-mail: admin@knittingfever.com URL: www.knittingfever.com

Acknowledgements

This book is dedicated to Stephen Jessup.
In the words of Paul Weller, 'I've searched the secret mists, I've climbed the highest peaks, And caught the wild wind home.'
Together, Forever, True love.

Thank you Stephen, for your wonderful photographs and for being my rock. I also thank our children,
Belle and Oscar, thankfully, children change everything. My wonderful family is always an inspiration and are always on hand for
support and guidance. I would also like to thank the whole team at Knitting Fever: Sion Elalouf, who believed in me and gave me the
exciting opportunity of launching my own yarn line, and also Jay, Jeff, and Haydee, who are always there and happy to help.

This book would not be possible without the help of my wonderful knitters, Betty Rothwell, Mrs. Marsh,
Amanda Mears, Mary Potter and my amazing mum, Daphne Harding.
I would like to thank the beautiful models: Charly Wright and Jennifer Lumb.

Thank you to Liz Rochford and Claire Salter for being such wonderfully creative make-up and hair artists, Innes Fairley and Emma
Wright for being such accommodating assistants and the staff at Cannon Hall, Cawthorne, where this book was photographed.
For great pattern-checking support I would like to thank Christopher Bahls.

Finally, thank you to Trisha Malcolm, Joy Aquilino and the fantastic team at Sixth&Spring Books
for their support, understanding and encouragement in the exciting realization and transformation
of an idea to a beautiful book.